Wesleyan Leadership
in Troubled Times

Other books by David L. McKenna:

The Urban Crisis (1968)

Awake, My Conscience (1977) (reprinted as *Contemporary Issues for Evangelical Christians*)

The Jesus Model (1978)

The Communicator's Commentary: Mark (1982)

MegaTruth: The Church in the Age of Information (1986)

Power to Follow: Grace to Lead: Strategy for the Future of Christian Leadership (1986)

The Communicator's Commentary: Job (1986)

Renewing Our Ministry (1986)

The Whisper of His Grace (1987)

Discovering Job (1989)

Love Your Work (1989)

The Coming Great Awakening (1990)

When Our Parents Need Us Most (1994)

The Communicator's Commentary: Isaiah 1—39 (1994)

The Communicator's Commentary: Isaiah 40—66 (1994)

A Future with a History: The Wesleyan Witness of the Free Methodist Church (1997)

Growing Up in Christ (1998)

Journey Through a Bypass: The Story of an Open Heart (1998)

What a Time to Be Wesleyan! (1999)

How to Read a Christian Book (2001)

The Christian Family Library. 37 volumes. General Editor (2002)

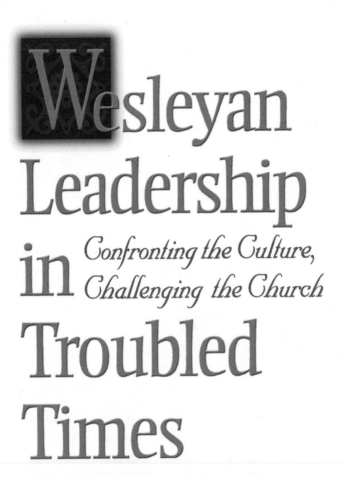

Wesleyan Leadership in

Confronting the Culture,
Challenging the Church

Troubled Times

David L. McKenna

Beacon Hill Press of Kansas City
Kansas City, Missouri

Copyright 2002
by Beacon Hill Press of Kansas City

ISBN 083-411-9579

Printed in the
United States of America

Cover Design: Michael Walsh

Library of Congress Cataloging-in-Publication-Data

McKenna, David L. (David Loren), 1929-
  Wesleyan leadership in troubled times : confronting the culture, challenging the church / David L. McKenna.
    p. cm.
Includes bibliographical references.
  ISBN 0-8341-1957-9 (pbk.)
 1. Christian leadership—Methodist Church. 2. Wesley, John, 1703-1791. I. Title.
  BX8349.L43 M35 2002
  262'.1—dc21

  2002002200

10 9 8 7 6 5 4 3 2 1

Contents

Prologue
Our Leading Edge

At exactly 2:31 P.M. in the afternoon of April 21, 2001, I heard the roar of a runaway train bearing down on our home. Having heard a similar sound as a child growing up in the Midwest, I yelled, "Tornado." My feet went out from under me. Like a drunken sailor trying to walk on a lurching ship, I staggered out of my study and met my wife who had just been thrown against the wall of the hallway. This time I yelled "Earthquake" and yanked her under the nearest archway. Hugging for dear life, we did a drunken sailor's dance on the rolling floor while walls creaked, windows rattled, and books fell. My journal now includes the entry

"Today, Jan and I survived an earthquake—7.3 on the Richter scale—Thank You, Lord."

We live on a fault line in Seattle. This is a crack running deep into the earth where horizontal plates rumble against each other and create a tension that continues to build until it must be released by violent eruption. When this happens, the surface breaks open and the landscape is radically altered.

Physical earthquakes change landscapes; spiritual earthquakes change history. The Word of God warns us about cosmic clashes between the forces of good and evil. Like the Seattle earthquake, many of these clashes are deep within the core of the culture, building tension that will not be relieved until there is violent eruption on the surface. When it happens, the landscape of history is dramatically changed.

If we listen carefully, we can hear the rumbling of spiritual conflict deep within the core of our culture. Tension is building between the glorification of the Radical Self and the glorification of the holy God. Only one of these forces can be dominant in the culture, and only one can be pervasive throughout the culture. Currently, the Radical Self appears to be winning. Secular scholars themselves identify self-interest as the dominant force that is shaping American character and the pervasive force that is influencing American culture.

Into this scene step Christian leaders of the Wesleyan tradition. Responsibility rests on our shoulders for a counterforce that will contend for the sovereignty of the holy God and the pervasive influence of biblical holiness among His people. A pitched battle is inevitable. On the front lines must be Wesleyan clergy and laity who take the risks of leadership because of our biblical identity, our missional convictions, our theological heritage, and our prophetic calling.

OUR BIBLICAL IDENTITY

Definitions of leadership are as plentiful as the number of volumes on leadership that crowd the business section in our bookstores. These definitions range from the simplicity of Peter Drucker's statement that "leaders are persons with followers" to the research-based conclusion of Roach and Behling that leadership "is the process of influencing an organized group toward accomplishing its goals." Christian writers tend to work off the same definitions while adding an emphasis upon character, citing biblical examples, and relating the results to redemptive outcomes. For the purposes of this book, our working definition will focus on the interaction between the biblical qualities of a leader and the response of those who are learning to lead. Leadership development, then, is the process of modeling and mentoring that comes through this interaction. Based on that understanding of biblical leadership, we offer this definition:

A biblical leader has a *God-given vision* that engages our commitment, a *Christlike character* that earns our trust, and a *Spirit-guided agenda* that mobilizes our energies.

Wesleyan leaders identify with all other Christian leaders in this definition. But there is more. We also need to ground our ministry in our missional convictions, take advantage of our Wesleyan heritage, and advance a working agenda for biblical holiness that gives distinction to our prophetic task.

Results-Driven Leadership. Where are the "results" or "outcomes" in this definition of biblical leadership? This is a natural question at a time when leaders are being called into accountability for the outcomes of their performance. Anyone who is acquainted with my history of educational leadership knows that I put a premium on performance for myself as well as for others. Annually, at the start of the academic year, I gave an address to the assembled college, university, or seminary community in which I announced my presidential goals for the year. At midyear, I reported on our progress toward those goals and, at the final faculty meeting of the year, invited evaluation of my leadership based on the achievement of those goals.

Why, then, do I not refer to "results, outcomes, and goals" in this definition of biblical leadership? Several reasons back up my decision. One is the belief that leadership development is defined as a qualitative process more than a quantitative product. While end results are in the mind of the biblical leader, they do not become a compulsion driving his or her ministry. The recent history of televangelists is a sordid reminder of what happens when the end justifies the means.

Another reason why I do not mention results is that this emphasis can be a concession to a secular definition of leadership. How often do we use the cliché of the "bottom line" in discussing the responsibility of leaders? The term comes directly from the corporate world, where leadership is ultimately judged by profits based on earnings and growth. Christian leaders have been seduced by this same motive. Think about the brag points that Christian leaders employ when they get together with colleagues. In response to the question "How are things going?" the answer becomes a contest in growth statistics. As the numbers escalate, the leader who cannot compete will resort to projections of potential gains or blame a downturn on uncontrollable forces. Without retreating behind the old saw that "we would rather be pure than big," our leadership development needs to be defined by our integrity and our faithfulness rather than the numbers on the "bottom line."

Most important of all, I do not mention results because biblical leadership is dependent upon the work of the Holy Spirit. Results-driven leadership tends to rely on human effort for its success. The penetrating words of John Stott at the 1974 Lausanne Congress on Evangelism still speak to this tendency. With the lofty vision of winning the world for Christ foremost in the minds of the delegates, Stott stopped us in our tracks when he said that we are only called to be faithful to our evangelistic task; the results belong to the work of the Holy Spirit. This truth is easily forgotten in a time when the techniques of leadership promise to close the gap between our efforts and our success so that the Holy Spirit is left out. When this happens, we distort the "Go, make, baptize, and teach" process of the Great Commission into a number count about which we can brag. We are already living with that distortion in statistics from across the world that show evangelism as our greatest strength but discipling as our greatest weakness. In our denominations, for example, if our converts were discipled into the measure of spiritual maturity implied by full church membership, the statistics of decline would be radically reversed.

Our case is made by the authority of God's Word in Acts 2:42-47 that serves as the benchmark for a biblical church. We immediately identify with the functions of preaching, teaching, worship, and fellowship, along with the spirit of praise and compassion for all. But we cannot overlook the concluding truth, *"And the Lord added to their number daily those who were being saved."* (Acts 2:47, emphasis added). Biblical leadership, whether in the 1st or 21st century, leaves the results in the hands of God.

OUR MISSIONAL CONVICTIONS

Implicit in the title of this book, *Wesleyan Leadership in Troubled Times: Confronting the Culture, Challenging the Church,* are three missional convictions. The first is the conviction that *biblical holiness is a timeless and universal truth that still sparks our imagination and engages our commitment.* Biblical holiness has many definitions and many nuances on those definitions. John Wesley himself used such terms as "perfection," "holiness," "entire sanctification," "perfect love," and "full salvation" interchangeably to describe what he also called the "fullness of faith." While controversy swirled around the meaning, timing, and sequence of this work of grace, Wesley never wavered in his affirmation of the doctrine, experience, and practice of biblical holiness: "This it is to be a perfect man, to be 'sanctified throughout;' even 'to have a heart so all-flaming with the love of God,' (to use Archbishop Usher's words), 'as continually to offer up every thought, word, and work, as a spiritual sacrifice, acceptable to God through Christ.'"[1]

Because this definition is consistent with biblical revelation, it is timeless across generations. Is it too much to expect that spiritual maturity in our generation still means "love excluding sin, love filling the heart, taking up the whole capacity of the soul"?[2] Or dare we believe that "faith working through love" is still the all-consuming motive for the heirs of the people called Methodists. "Be holy for I am holy" is as much God's command for 21st-century Christians as it was for 1st-century Christians. Furthermore, biblical holiness is "culture free." Whether the setting is the prosperous, high-tech Western world or the impoverished, primitive two-thirds world, the truth of biblical holiness still holds.

The second missional conviction undergirding this book is that *biblical holiness is a truth that sets us apart as Wesleyan leaders and holds us together as a Wesleyan family.* In the scramble for identity among denominations, Wesleyans do not need to search for a distinctive. The unity of personal and social holiness is a "given" from biblical revelation, church history, denominational identity, and contemporary need. To date, however, we have spent more time looking back upon our history, defining terms, and defending a shrinking position than projecting forward an agenda that makes biblical holiness our pervasive principle. For the future, we must see biblical holiness as our "binding address," a term coined by Robert Bellah and his colleagues in the book *Habits of the Heart.* By their definition, a binding address functions as a moral ecology that is "the web of moral understandings and commitments that tie people together in community."[3] A binding address, then, is vision based on moral conviction that pervades every phase of a society, is shared by its people, and gives that society its cohesion. If this same definition is applied to our Wesleyan world today, it means that biblical holiness is a spiritual conviction that pervades every phase of our ministry, claims the commitment of every member, and serves as the glue that holds us together. It also gives our leadership agenda its distinctive quality and its cohesive nature. In biblical holiness, we find the binding address by which we are known, by which we become one, and by which we lead.

Our third missional conviction is that *biblical holiness is our promise for wholeness and hope.* We are a "generation of seekers" on a spiritual quest for wholeness and hope. The quest, however, is like Walt Whitman's "noiseless, patient spider," spinning out filaments into thin air hoping that one will catch so that the security of a web can be built. In response to that futile search, the Wesleyan message of biblical holiness not only promises wholeness and hope but also has been proven in practice. The Wesleyan story is replete with the testimonies of individuals, the records of churches, and the history of cultures as witness to the wholeness and hope that come with the outpouring of God's Holy Spirit. The 21st century is no exception. Our need is obvious, and God's promise is sure. As the Wesleyan message of wholeness and hope has been written in the annals of history, it will be written again in our generation.

Our Wesleyan Heritage

In the book *What a Time to Be Wesleyan!* I wrote that those of us who share the heritage of John Wesley have an advantage for leadership in changing and tumultuous times. Because of our confidence in the continuing work of the Holy Spirit in our world, we are called to lead when truth is on the scaffold, ambiguity is on the throne, and anxiety rules the times. Wesley had a gift for holding truth in suspension and bringing it into balance when other theologians came down hard on one side or the other. Calvinist theologians, for instance, put such emphasis on the sovereignty of God that they sacrificed the freedom of our God-given nature. Through the mind of the Spirit, Wesley made room for human freedom in the plan of salvation without sacrificing the sovereignty of the holy God. Likewise, in his view of biblical holiness, he did not fall into the error of making a second work of grace an end in itself. Spiritual growth, both before and after the experience, was essential to the doctrine.

Perhaps more than ever before, Wesleyan leaders in the 21st-century world must have the mind of the Spirit in order to the deal with paradox, conflict, and ambiguity. Philip Yancey addresses this need in his book *The Invisible God.* He quotes G. K. Chesterton, who said, "Christianity got over the difficulty of combining furious opposites by keeping them both, and keeping them furious."[4] What a description for authentic Wesleyan leadership! "Furious opposites" describe the context within which we must lead in the new millennium. The Wesleyan quadrilateral is a prime example. "Furious opposites" make up the essence of Wesleyan theology—revelation, reason, experience, and tradition. A moment's reflection shows a continuing contest at each of these points. Revelation is forced into the opposites of narrow inerrancy or private interpretation; reason is pushed to the extremes of theological arrogance or anti-intellectual reaction; experience is divided between ecstatic excesses and casual commitments; and tradition suffers from being suspect as a barrier to progress or a defensive shield against change.

In dealing with all four sides of the quadrilateral, Wesley is known for his uncanny ability to bring balance to "furious opposites." His native intellect gave him a head start on this quality of leadership, but only his obedience to the mind of the Holy Spirit could bring a creative and constructive balance to the issues he faced. Wesleyan leaders today must be equally attentive to the cultivation of intellect and obedient to the mind of the Holy Spirit. Task descriptions should be written for Wesleyan leaders of the 21st century before they are elected or appointed. Like the task descriptions for the seven deacons elected by the Early Church, their qualifications would include being "full of the Spirit and wisdom" (Acts 6:3). Their character would be affirmed by the fullness of the Spirit, and their competencies would be attested by their practical wisdom. Certainly, high among those competencies requiring wisdom would be their "demonstrated ability to lead through the paradox of truth, conflict of convictions, and ambiguity of choices." As the seven deacons had their character and competence put to test immediately after their election in the 1st century, Wesleyan leadership in the 21st century will rise or fall on the same qualifications.

OUR PROPHETIC TASK

Leaders who claim to be prophets are victims of self-delusion. Yet leaders who deny their prophetic task are remiss in their responsibilities. C. L. Franklin has written, "A prophet has sight, insight and foresight. With sight he looks on things. With insight he looks into things. With foresight he looks beyond things."[5] In order to see the vision for biblical holiness and make it our binding address, Wesleyan leaders must take on this prophetic role. Consequently, the outline for this book follows this sequence of "sight, insight, and foresight."

Our approach in Part I: The Sight of Reality will be to gain a perspective for understanding the present by retracing the Great Awakenings in American history. These events have been defining moments that continue to shape our character and our culture. Reality will come to us with full force when we realize that we are called to lead and serve in what will be known as the Fourth Great Awakening in American history and its aftermath of troubled times.

Part II: The Insight of Truth will probe into that reality as we look at the spiritual challenges coming out of the Fourth Great Awakening, particularly for biblical holiness as defined by Scripture, advanced by our Wesleyan forefathers, and incumbent upon us today.

Part III: The Foresight of Hope will be a call for Wesleyan leaders to activate a Spirit-guided agenda that both sets us apart and holds us together. Admittedly, this is a large order. With biblical identity for our leadership, missional convictions as our base, Wesleyan theology as our heritage, and a Spirit-guided agenda as our prophetic task, the prospect of "faith working through love" is a promise waiting to be fulfilled in our generation.

Our thoughts will come to conclusion in the Epilogue: Our Living Hope where we recognize that prophetic leaders communicate with their followers through a keen sense of timing. The gift of expectancy that characterized the apostolic leaders is the gift that still sets prophetic leaders apart. How is that gift exercised in leadership today? The answer awaits the epilogue.

PART I

The Sight of Reality

For this is my prayer: that your love may abound more and more in knowledge and depth of insight, so that you may be able to discern what is best and may be pure and blameless until the day of Christ, filled with the fruits of righteousness that comes through Jesus Christ—to the glory and praise of God.

—Philippians 1:9-11

The first responsibility of a leader is to define reality.

—Max DuPree

1 The Four Great Awakenings

 The "sight" of a prophet comes into focus in Max De-Pree's definition of a leader when he writes, "The first responsibility of a leader is to define reality."[1] This is no easy task. To define reality requires a "big picture" perspective. Like a star athlete who has the advantage of extraordinary peripheral vision to see the whole field or floor upon which the game takes place, a prophetic leader sees the field for spiritual action along the sightlines of history and through the scope of present reality. Too often contemporary leadership is flawed by the limited scope of tunnel vision or the limited depth of historical understanding. Whoever said that "many contemporary leaders have failed to read the minutes of the last meeting" struck at the heart of the issue. To define contemporary reality, a leader must have a keen sense of history. So, like the flight of Robert Benchley's fabled "killey-doo" bird, we must take off backward to see where we have been before we can turn forward to see where we are going.

A FRESH LOOK AT SPIRITUAL REALITY

Ever since I can remember, Christian leaders have been praying for a great spiritual awakening in our world. What if God has answered our prayers and we are living in the midst of the Fourth Great Awakening in American history? Suddenly, our responsibility for the definition of reality would change. Christian leadership in the midst of spiritual awakening is different from Christian leadership calling for spiritual awakening. If it is a fact that we are being called to lead *in the midst* of the Fourth Great Awakening in American history, our first responsibility as leaders is to define reality within this context.

GREAT AWAKENINGS IN AMERICAN HISTORY

To refresh our memories, let me offer a brief vignette for each of the four Great Awakenings in American history. Admittedly, these word pictures are sketchy and not without dispute among historians. Nevertheless, they give us the "sight of reality" that we need for "insight into the truth" and "foresight into the future."

Keep in mind these ground rules when reading these vignettes. First, Great Awakenings are identified only when spiritual revival results in social reform. A revival in the church without reform in the culture cannot be considered a Great Awakening. Second, it takes a full generation or more before a spiritual revival results in social reform. Time is needed for the moral influence of a Great Awakening to course its way in the heart of the culture and transform society. Third, although Great Awakenings are identified by periods, they overlap in time and impact. No event in history stands alone without roots in the past and shoots into the future. Great Awakenings, especially, merge together throughout American history. Fourth, although Great Awakenings reflect the differences of their times, they show common characteristics that help us understand and anticipate them. Historians are always reluctant to read the future into the past or to force human events into predictive patterns. At the same time, they do not deny the insights that are gained from a perspective of history that sees discernible trends, overlapping movements, and repetitions of behavior. We need that perspective in order to understand the Great Awakenings in American history.

After presenting these "sight bites" of the four Great Awakenings, our viewpoint will be presented in a chart that shows the common components of spiritual events that are part and parcel of our national history.

THE FIRST GREAT AWAKENING
1740s to 1780s

The First Great Awakening in American history began in the 1740s under the leadership of Jonathan Edwards and George Whitefield. Whitefield, the English evangelist, brought with him from his homeland the influence of John Wesley and the spirit of the Wesleyan revival. We see that influence in the two impulses that followed the conversion of the masses in the eastern colonies. One impulse stimulated the Christian spirit of "disinterested benevolence" that led the church and its believers into ministries for the poor, the sick, the aged, and the homeless. Out of this impulse came the establishment of hospitals, orphanages, schools, and homes for the needy without discrimination. As a natural response of the redeemed soul, the evidence of "disinterested benevolence" still serves as a benchmark for the evidence of a Great Awakening.

A companion impulse of that First Great Awakening was a sense of redemptive freedom for the society as well as for the individual. Out of this impulse of redemptive freedom came the motivation for *political equality*. People who are free in Christ cannot be bound by the chains of oppression. Christian leaders, however, are not immediately identified with rebellion against the king of England. Revolutionary coalitions led by Deists, such as Thomas Jefferson and Alexander Hamilton, adopted this impulse for their own even as they cut its biblical roots. A full generation went by before the colonies won their independence from the English monarchy in 1776. Yet, as the history of the First Great Awakening comes full cycle, we see the fires of spiritual freedom fueling the flame of political freedom.

THE SECOND GREAT AWAKENING
1840s to 1870s

While it takes a full generation for a Great Awakening to cycle from spiritual revival to social reform, it also takes only a generation for the moral vitality of revival to be lost. This is particularly true when the roots of biblical truth are cut and coalitions of nonbelievers adopt the cause without the source. By the end of the 18th century, for instance, the influence of French Deism had become a dominant force in the new nation. Once again, intellectual skepticism and moral corruption took over the culture. What some historians consider the Second Great Awakening began in the 1790s when spiritual revival under the leadership of Timothy Dwight, president of Yale, swept through the college and then through the churches, the communities, and into the eastern states of the new nation.

Following that same spirit of revival into the opening decades of the 19th century, Francis Asbury engaged an army of circuit riders who took the message of Christ to the Western frontier. The social impact of that revival movement is noted by Nathan Hatch in his book *The Democratization of the American Christianity*. Hatch credits the camp meeting movement as a major factor in bringing the

Eastern seaboard and the Western frontier together under the bond of a new symbol for unity, "One nation under God."[2]

Wider recognition of a Second Great Awakening, however, is given to spiritual revival that had its genesis in the 1840s under the evangelistic thrust of Charles Finney. Just as Timothy Dwight found no conflict in being a fervent advocate for the faith and a distinguished academic leader, Finney also served as president of Oberlin College while pursuing his evangelistic ministry. Converts of Finney, particularly in the newly developing cities, felt the impulse of redemptive freedom with both its personal and social consequences that we saw evidenced in the First Great Awakening. Not only did they embrace a strong work ethic that took them out of the chains of the urban ghetto, but they also took the lead in addressing the needs of those who were victims of a society in transition. Child labor laws complemented by compulsory education in public schools with a strong biblical and moral base topped the social priorities on the Evangelical agenda. Christian leaders championed women's rights and gave leadership to the beginning of the suffrage movement. But opposition to human slavery stood as the centerpiece for redemptive freedom in the Second Great Awakening. History records that out of the impulse of spiritual revival came the drive for *social equality*. Spiritual freedom is always incompatible with the chains of slavery, oppression, or discrimination.

While some daring Christian leaders were carrying their case against slavery, coalitions of abolitionists co-opted their agenda and politicized the slavery issue without acknowledging its redemptive roots. It took the troubling times of the Civil War to resolve the issue, but the Emancipation Proclamation stands as another landmark for freedom in our nation. Because a full generation passed from the beginning of the Second Great Awakening in the 1840s and the end of the Civil War in 1865, the redemptive impulse for social freedom could have been forgotten. The life histories of Evangelical Christian leaders and the stories of Wesleyan and Holiness movements show otherwise. The redemptive impulse of the Second Great Awakening qualifies as a major impetus for social reform leading to freedom for the slaves. The same redemptive impulse set America apart as the nation in which voluntary social agencies were established to meet the needs of the poor, the sick, and the homeless. The Red Cross, the United Way, the YMCA, and the YWCA—all trace their beginnings to that era with credit to spiritual renewal as the genesis for human compassion.

THE THIRD GREAT AWAKENING
1880s to 1950s

Social crisis is seen again toward the end of the 19th century when industrial development caused the dislocation of millions of agriculture workers as they made adjustments to the factory system. Adding to the crisis, immigrants of Roman Catholic faith poured into the teeming cities in search of factory jobs. At the same time, the credibility of the Christian came under attack when the influence of the German enlightenment swept through the universities and challenged biblical authority. Out of this conflicting climate and troubled times, the Third Great Awakening began in the 1880s when Dwight Moody took his evangelistic message to university campuses. Spiritual revival followed, not just on public university campuses but also in the culture at large.

The Holiness Movement was a powerful force that overlapped the Second and Third Great Awakenings. The experience of "perfect love" for the human heart matched the vision for a "more perfect union" in the rising nation. Holiness leaders not only spoke the dream of a Christian nation but became advocates of social reform on such issues as labor unions, tax reform, higher education, and women's rights. B. T. Roberts, the founder of the Free Methodist Church, for instance, risked his leadership by advocating these reforms at the same time that he was an impassioned evangelist who preached the experiences of personal justification and entire sanctification.

Economic equality became the touchstone for the Third Great Awakening as its spiritual impulse was co-opted for a political agenda. Fulfilling the millennial vision of a Christian nation but cut from its redemptive roots, economic equality was foreseen as the outcome for all people in the newly developing industrial and urban nation. At this point, American history enters a great divide. When liberal theologians usurped the biblical vision and declared the 20th century as the "Christian Century," Evangelicals retreated from their agenda for social reform and turned their energies toward world evangelism. Advocates of a Social Gospel became the new millennialists who saw salvation in social reform rather than personal redemption. Borrowing the Holiness vision for a Christian nation without its theological roots, they carried their agenda into legislative action that culminated in the creation of the welfare state in the 1930s and eventually, into the Great Society of the 1960s.

THE FOURTH GREAT AWAKENING
1970s to the Present

Although historians tell us that it takes at least 75 years before you can make a final judgment on the past, there is good reason to believe that we are in the midst of another Great Awakening at this time. If so, we cannot wait for 75 years and forfeit our responsibility as Christian leaders to seek the insight of truth into the sight of reality.

Fogel uses the term "the Fourth Great Awakening" without apology in his book by the same title.[3] I, too, in my book, found evidence that the Born-Again Movement of the mid-1970s represented a spiritual revival of proportions not unlike those seen in the Great Awakenings of the past. When estimates of the number of people who claim to be Bible-believing, born-again Christians range from 40 to 60 million, their impact upon history cannot be ignored. Without apology, I, too, declare that we are living in the first full generation since the beginning of the Fourth Great Awakening.

The prelude for this awakening began in the social crisis of the 1960s when our society spun out of control because of the shock of the Kennedy assassinations, the civil-rights related violence, the campus riots, the Vietnam War, Woodstock, and political protest. During this time, Billy Graham gained international prominence and Evangelical Christianity moved into the mainstream of national influence. Conversely, liberal Christians who championed the Social Gospel found themselves embracing a bankrupt theology. While the welfare state they espoused brought large measures of economic and educational equity to the society, neither benefit changed the hearts of the people. Quite to the contrary, moral corruption has become our greatest concern and personal violence our greatest fear.

As its predecessors of spiritual awakening in the past, the Born-Again Movement of the mid-1970s took a quick turn into the political arena. Rather than following the path of the first three Great Awakenings into benevolence for the poor and disenfranchised, the redemptive impulse of the Fourth Great Awakening turned back toward the recovery of a moral society through political action. Led by its pro-life and pro-family agenda, the Moral Majority had a direct influence on the election of Ronald Reagan as a conservative president. "Traditional values" now became the watchword for legislative action pointing toward moral recovery. Reversal of *Roe v. Wade*, prayer in public schools, opposition to violence in the media, support for capital punishment, and enforcement of drug laws joined the Republican platform of supply-side economics and tax relief as the path toward a moral and prosperous nation. This agenda, however, was short-circuited at the center of power with the election of Bill Clinton as president in 1992. Campaigning on a political platform that countered most of these conservative initiatives, Clinton hardened the lines of conflict and then increased the gulf with his own moral downfall.

Almost a full generation after the spiritual revival of the Born-Again Movement, Robert Fogel contends that the equity principle of redemptive freedom is still at work. In the First Great Awakening, *political equality* was the driving force; in the Second Great Awakening, it was *social equality*; in the Third, *economic equality*. Now, as Fogel contends, that each of these needs is met in large measure by a free and prosperous society, the drive is for *spiritual equity*.[4] In other words, Fogel says that we need the spiritual resources for "self-actualization," a hybrid term that combines the psychological hierarchy of Abraham Maslow with the theological promise of redemptive potential. Or to put it another way, a large majority of North Americans have their needs for political, social, and economic freedom met, but they still suffer from the poverty of spiritual despair. An observation of the Republican and Democrat parties in the United States tends to confirm this idea. While their political, social, and economic platforms are worlds apart, each has moved to a centrist position on moral and spiritual matters. Both recognize the need for the recovery of families, morality in the media, the control of substance abuse, the reduction of violence, and improvements in health care. Both also stand together on the commitment to provide spiritual leadership for bringing together an increasingly diverse nation. Although the jury is still out on the outcomes of the Fourth Great Awakening, there is no doubt about its role in shaping the character and culture of our society.

SPIRITUAL REALITY: AN OVERVIEW

Sketchy as they are, these vignettes give us an overview of spiritual reality that prophetic leaders must understand and within which they must work. Both the scope and the depth of that reality is seen in the following chart:

Several observations come to mind as we see the Four Great Awakenings in this larger perspective.

CHART I
GREAT AWAKENINGS IN AMERICAN HISTORY

	HUMAN NEED:	EVANGELIST:	THEOLOGICAL CONFLICT:	PUBLIC ISSUES:	SOCIAL GOAL:
FIRST GREAT AWAKENING 1740s-1770s	Freedom from Tyranny	George Whitefield	Personal vs. Impersonal God	Human Rights Corrupt Governance	Political Equality
SECOND GREAT AWAKENING 1840s-1870s	Freedom from Slavery	Charles Finney	Class vs. Human Rights	Slavery Temperance Child Labor Public Education Women's Suffrage	Social Equality
THIRD GREAT AWAKENING 1880s— 1930s	Freedom from Poverty	Dwight Moody	Individual vs. Social Salvation	Immigration Higher Education Labor Unions Civil Rights	Economic Equality
FOURTH GREAT AWAKENING 1970s-Present	Freedom from Despair	Billy Graham	Absolute vs. Relative Truth	Abortion Family Values Feminism Gay Rights Gambling/ Drugs Media Violence	Spiritual Equality

- Spiritual awakenings have played a major role in the writing of American history.
- God has anointed evangelists as leaders of spiritual awakenings in each generation.

- Redemption through Jesus Christ begins with individual freedom and carries over into issues of social freedom.
- In each generation, spiritual awakenings take place in the midst of social, theological, and political conflict.
- Spiritual awakenings have been major contributors to the march of American democracy toward equality for all.
- Most important of all, spiritual awakenings are not unmixed blessings. Although individuals are redeemed, institutions are reformed, and society is renewed, spiritual awakenings are neither perpetual nor assured in any generation. In fact, as the cycle of history turns, there is a falling away from the high tide of a spiritual awakening as its energy is lost in the church, its theological roots are cut by scholars, and its redemptive freedom is usurped by political forces.

2 The Cycles of Great Awakenings

 Does human history turn in cycles? The answer is debatable. Some scholars take a linear view of history. From their perspective, the events of history march in sequence along a straight line. A thread of continuity may connect current events with the past and the future, but there is no cycle of events that is repetitive of past history or predictive of future history. Other scholars see human history moving through definite cycles. While avoiding the error of suggesting that the future is predetermined by the past, these scholars still find commonalities in historical generations that suggest cycles in the turn of events. Following the adage "He who does not learn from history is condemned to repeat it," these scholars ask us to learn from the past and apply that learning as an opportunity to shape the future.

CYCLICAL THEORIES OF HISTORY

Foremost among the scholars holding a cyclical view of history was Oswald Spengler, who wrote *The Decline of the West*. Spengler's book is one of the most widely read histories of all time and is invariably included on any list of great books in Western civilization. His writing, however, is not without controversy. Rejecting linear progression as the approach to history, Spengler advanced an organic view in which civilizations follow a life cycle. They spring up like seeds from the soil, come to full bloom, and then die as their life-giving resources are exhausted. When he applied the cyclical metaphor to Western civilization, Spengler perceived the evidence of decline already at work. With Goethe and Hegel as his intellectual mentors, he viewed the rise of the Nazi regime as proof of that decline.

Spengler's cycle of civilization leads us to ask another question. *Does our spiritual history also turn on cycles?* Again, the answer is debatable. Theologically, the linear viewpoint of spiritual history tends to dominate the thinking of most Evangelical Christians. Premillennialists, postmillennialists, amillennialists—all see spiritual history as a linear progression. The difference is the direction of the straight line. Premillennialists view spiritual history declining on a straight line downward toward the apocalypse, with the second coming of Christ intervening. Postmillennialists take the opposite viewpoint. For them, spiritual history is rising on a straight line upward toward the fulfillment of the kingdom of God on earth, following which Christ shall come. Amillennialists reject both extremes in favor of a straight line moving horizontally toward the Second Coming without making judgment on its rising or falling action because Jesus himself said that only the Father knows when He will come again.

Among these viewpoints, popularity belongs to the premillennialists, especially those who are identified as dispensationalists. In their view of spiritual history, dispensationalists not only see a straight line declining toward doom but also interpret biblical prophecy by periods of time and events that are predictable and inevitable. Hal Lindsey's book *The Late Great Planet Earth* is the contemporary lodestar for dispensationalism. Published in the 1970s, it became the best-selling book in both secular and religious markets for the decade. Now, in the 21st century, fictionalized versions of dispensationalism have taken center stage in the book markets. Beginning with the novel *Left Behind*, Tim LaHaye and Jerry Jenkins have written a succession of volumes that sell by the millions across secular and religious markets. While open to the criticism that these books both play on the fears of nonbelievers who feel as if our world is spinning out of control and reduce the need for mature faith among believers, their widespread influence cannot be denied.

THE CYCLE OF THE SPIRIT

Among the options presented by these differing viewpoints, our choice is to take a cyclical view of spiritual history and an amillennial stance on the direction of that history. This choice is not new. Biblical scholars have seen cycles of apostasy, revival, and renewal prefigured in the prophecies of Scripture, and Church historians have traced these cycles through the ages. For example, Joel prophesied, "In the last days, God says, I will pour out my Spirit on all people. Your sons and daughters will prophesy, your young men will see visions, your old men will dream dreams. Even on my servants, both men and women, I will pour out my Spirit in those days, and they will prophesy" (Acts 2:17-18; see Joel 2:28-29).

When Peter took this prophecy as his text to describe the happenings at Pentecost, he may have envisioned the end of time and the imminent return of Jesus Christ. But when it didn't happen, the prophecy became the promise for the outpouring of the Holy Spirit from time to time in the development of the infant Church. Church historians now see this same promise fulfilled again and again throughout the ages as Christians pray for revival, renewal, and reform in each generation. Joel's promise holds for us today. Through the outpouring of the Holy Spirit, we see hope for our world.

THE CYCLE OF GREAT AWAKENINGS

Both secular and religious scholars see the four Great Awakenings in American history as representative of spiritual cycles. Historian Timothy Smith, in his classic work *Revivalism and Social Reform*,[1] sees the impact of spiritual awakening upon the culture as well as the Church. William McLoughlin advances Smith's work with additional insights in his scholarly work *Revivals, Awakenings, and Reform*.[2] Complementing these historical studies, Anthony F. C. Wallace looks at Great Awakenings from the perspective of a sociologist and sees in them a five-stage cycle of revitalization: (1) steady state, (2) individual stress, (3) cultural distortion, (4) revitalization, and (5) a new steady state.[3]

Evangelical Christian scholars have applied these historical and sociological insights to their understanding of our spiritual history. Richard Lovelace, in his book *Dynamics of Spiritual Life: An Evangelical Theology of Renewal*,[4] blends biblical theology with cultural anthropology to view spiritual awakenings as continuous, cyclical, and supernatural. Howard Snyder, in *Signs of the Spirit*, writes that the life of the Church rises and falls, "not in static, linear terms, but as dynamic, living, and fluctuating."[5] In my book *The Coming Great Awakening* I combine these biblical, historical, and sociological understandings into a framework that emphasizes the role of Christian students on college campuses as past, present, and future leaders of spiritual awakenings in the Church and the society at large.

With the turn into the 21st century, the interest of secular authors is again piqued by the cyclical theory of history, including Great Awakenings. Although economics is dubbed as the "dismal science," it is a Nobel prize-winning economist named Robert William Fogel who has written the book *The Fourth Great Awakening and the Future of Egalitarianism*.[6] Fogel sends shock waves through the academy when he identifies Evangelicals as the leaders for the Great Awakenings in American history who have advanced the cause of democracy and who hold the promise for egalitarianism in the future. Other advocates of a cyclical theory of history are not so optimistic. *The Fourth Turning: An American Prophecy,* by William Strauss and Neil Howe, is described as a "pseudoscholarly" text that plays on the same fears as dispensationalist prophecies but from a New Age and futurist perspective. According to the authors, the "first turning" was the "high" of optimism after World War II, the "second turning" was the "Consciousness Revolution" between 1964 and 1984, and the "third turning" was the "Culture Wars" from 1985 to 2005. Now the "fourth turning" is the "unraveling" of cohesive values that make up the common good so that a crisis of cataclysmic proportions is inevitable. Hence, from a secularist's point of view, the fourth turning illustrates the deterministic and doomsaying results when cyclical theory is taken to its extremes.[7]

To understand the Great Awakenings, we need to recall the cycle that is common to each of them. Anthony Wallace gives us the sociologist's viewpoint in his "revitalization theory." I, then, adapted his theory to a spiritual understanding of Great Awakenings with a focus on the role of Christian higher education as a source for revival. Let me describe this sequence as "The Spiritual Cycle of Great Awakenings," which results in social transformation through individual redemption.

THE SPIRITUAL CYCLE OF GREAT AWAKENINGS

A word of caution. We want to view the four Great Awakenings as cycles in American history that are neither predetermined nor pessimistic. In them we see a learning experience for believers with special emphasis upon their responsibility in this generation to revitalize the Church and the culture through the fresh outpouring of the Holy Spirit. Our learning begins with a review of the Spiritual Cycle, which can be detected in each of the four Great Awakenings in American history.

1. **Steady State.** From time to time a society comes to a period when there is general consensus on moral values and a balance between the competing demands of individual freedom and the common good. A look back to the vignettes of the four Great Awakenings suggests that these times have come following major wars that engaged the whole nation—the War of Independence, the Civil War,

CHART II
THE SPIRITUAL CYCLE OF GREAT AWAKENINGS

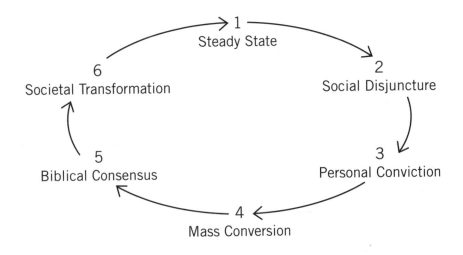

and World Wars I and II. Using the Fourth Great Awakening as an example, America went through a steady-state period following World War II in the Eisenhower administration. The era was characterized by euphoria when the American dream came back into view. Politically, it was carried on the public chant "I like Ike." Socially, we saw the prospect of equal opportunity for all our people. Morally, there was general consensus on traditional values regarding sex, marriage, and divorce. Educationally, public colleges and universities were seen as the panacea for social ills. Intellectually, the minds of students were as "quiet as mice." Spiritually, established churches were enjoying a resurgence of growth and commitment on the part of their members. Although this glossy idealism was short lived, we still look back on that era as the benchmark against which change is measured in the decades to follow.

   2. Social Disjuncture. Sooner or later, steady state is turned upside down by some form of rupture in the fabric of society. The disjunctures are often the result of technological change that upsets the security of the status quo, but they may also be the result of social crisis. An obvious example of technological change is seen in the Third Great Awakening in the late 1900s when the shift from an agricultural to an industrial economy forced people to the cities and brought in hordes of Irish Catholic immigrants to our shores. Or in the Fourth Great Awakening, the disjuncture was created by social forces, beginning with the assassination of John F. Kennedy, which shook to the core the moral base of the nation. A culture out of control creates desperate people.

3. **Personal Conviction.** When social disjuncture cannot be explained or controlled by human means, desperation settles into *personal conviction.* The sovereignty of God is recognized, and the reality of human sin is acknowledged. As a prelude to the First Great Awakening, for instance, Jonathan Edward's sermon "Sinners in the Hands of an Angry God" is often cited as the standard for personal conviction, but each Great Awakening has a moment of its own. In the cycle of the Fourth Great Awakening, Americans tried to use Richard Nixon's betrayal of trust as the scapegoat to carry away our sin. We failed because in the mirror of his sin we saw ourselves. Personal conviction gripped the nation.

4. **Mass Conversion.** Out of personal conviction, people turn to God. In each of the Great Awakenings, there is evidence of mass conversion as people repent of their sins. J. Edwin Orr, perhaps the best-known student of revival, tells us the story of the Welsh Revival. When the experience of conversion swept through the villages, so many Welsh miners came to Christ and changed their lives that the pit ponies in the mines could not understand their commands because they no longer laced their language with curses. No less dramatic was the spiritual movement in the 1970s when Gallup identified 40 million or more Americans who claimed to be "born-again, Bible-believing, and witnessing" Christians. Critics might downplay the connection between the traumatic years that preceded Gallup's surprising statistic. The timing, however, cannot be ignored. Out of the Born-Again Movement, Evangelical Christianity moved from the margins to the center of our society and became recognized as a significant moral and spiritual force.

5. **Biblical Consensus.** Personal redemption through Jesus Christ not only frees the converts from sin but also brings them to the Word of God as the final source of authority for their lives. Together, the experience of redemption and the authority of the Word create in them a *spirit of benevolence* for the poor and the needy. This ethic of benevolence generated by spiritual revival is the genius of the American commitment to the "common good." In the First Great Awakening, we saw the influence of George Whitefield who, although a Calvinist, was a colleague of John Wesley in the English revival. Wesley's emphasis upon personal and social holiness carried

over to the colonies as hospitals, orphanages, and schools were founded as a result of spiritual revival. The spirit of benevolence is still being formed in the Fourth Great Awakening. With great hope, we can see the results in examples of Evangelical Christians seeking racial reconciliation and showing leadership for the needs of the poor, sick, and homeless through "faith-based charities."

Out of the spirit of benevolence, a *biblical consensus* on moral issues is formed as the Evangelical agenda for social reform. In each of the Great Awakenings, the general spirit of benevolence becomes specific on contemporary issues of equality that address the needs of disenfranchised people. Although those needs vary in each generation, the Evangelical agenda of the Great Awakenings always has a heart for the poor, the sick, the homeless, the ignorant, the abused, and the disadvantaged.

6. **Social Transformation.** When the cycle of spiritual awakening turns full cycle, there is evidence of *social transformation* with roots in revival. Even though historians may disagree on the details, they concur that the democratic movement toward political, social, and economic equality over the past 300 years has been directly influenced by the motivation for freedom created by spiritual renewal. The jury is still out on the influence of the Fourth Great Awakening as a source for transformation in an affluent age and diverse culture where impoverishment is the lack of spiritual resources for self-actualization. But that is not the end of the story.

THE SECULAR CYCLE OF GREAT AWAKENINGS

A second look at the Great Awakenings reveals another cycle at work. In the past we stopped with the evidence of social transformation rooted in spiritual revival. Now we need to recognize a second cycle that begins where the Spiritual Cycle leaves off. To draw the contrast, let me label this sequence as "The Secular Cycle of Great Awakenings," in which reform takes place through political action. Chart III shows the turning of this cycle.

1. **Evangelical Agenda.** The Secular Cycle of Great Awakenings begins where the Spiritual Cycle ends. Out of the spirit of disinterested benevolence, an agenda for social reform is developed. Contemporary Christians might be surprised to learn that leaders of the Second Great Awakening, for instance, advocated the establishment of public schools, the rights of labor unions, and suffrage for women, as well as the abolition of slavery. In the Fourth Great Awaken-

CHART III
THE SECULAR CYCLE OF GREAT AWAKENINGS

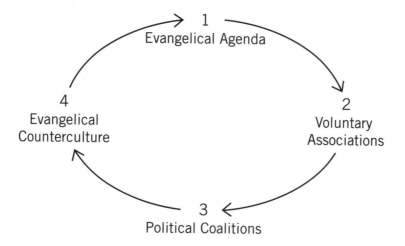

ing, we have already seen the social agenda of Evangelicals take on issues of abortion, gambling, homosexuality, and morality in the media, as well as family rights and values.

2. Voluntary Associations. In each Great Awakening, Evangelical leaders are out in front with an agenda that addresses the needs of the disenfranchised and the disadvantaged. Naturally, then, they spark the interest of political forces that see the opportunity to ride the spiritual passion of Evangelicals into their own agenda for social reform. Out of this motivation, *voluntary associations* arise with a single purpose platform adopted from the Evangelical agenda. These associations represent an intermediate step between an Evangelical spirit and a political action. They tend to be informal networks appealing to people who either feel disenfranchised or are advocates for the disenfranchised. The rise of revolutionaries, abolitionists, and millennialists in each of the first three Great Awakenings confirms this observation. Sad to say, however, the Evangelical agenda of disinterested benevolence is co-opted by *political interests* that tend to separate the motivation for action from its roots in spiritual revival. In the Fourth Great Awakening we are witness to the single-purpose groups that have found their cause in the redemptive freedom of the Born-Again Movement. The Moral Majority and Promise Keepers are examples of Evangelical organizations created from the motivation of the Fourth Great Awakening. They are not alone. Voluntary associations on the other side of the agenda have also been formed. The American Way, the National Organization for Women, and Greenpeace are now household names for networks of social protest.

3. Political Coalitions. As the motivation for social reform spreads, *political coalitions* are created out of diverse constituencies with a common cause. By now, however, the original Evangelical agenda may not even be recognized because these coalitions adopt a secular agenda and liberal platform in order to bring together groups that may historically be "cobelligerents" on other issues. In the Fourth Great Awakening, we see these coalitions forming around the issues of abortion, feminism, gay rights, and free-speech lobbies for the media industry. On the other side, the Christian Coalition is equally committed to political action against such issues as abortion and homosexuality, and in favor of legislation permitting prayer in the public schools as well as federal funding for faith-based charities. Political coalitions, whether on the Right or Left, inevitably increase polarization in a society.

4. Evangelical Counterculture. When the political coalitions are firmly entrenched in their positions, an *Evangelical counterculture* is created. Strange as it seems, the spiritual source for social transformation is now conceived as a nativistic movement looking backward to bygone days. In the public mind, for instance, Evangelicals are perceived to be synonymous with the religious Right, conspirators against freedom, advocates of discrimination, and calloused toward the needs of the disadvantaged and disenfranchised. At the other extreme, the religious Left has little to offer. Activists contending for such issues as free speech, environmentalism, economic equality, sexual preferences, and human rights have radicalized the religious Left's Social Gospel agenda. As already noted, Republican and Democratic parties are rejecting the extremes and moving toward the center on moral issues. Out of spiritual revival and the Evangelical agenda they are being drawn together around these common concerns—restoration of the family, morality in the media, tolerance in religious diversity, enforcement of drug laws, and protection for citizens against violence.

To say the least, the Secular Cycle of Great Awakenings ends in irony. From a beginning in spiritual revival, the cycle turns into a secular agenda of political coalitions that pushes Evangelicals into the identity of a counterculture. Even more ironic is the fact that the renewal of the moral and spiritual climate created by revival erodes again if the redemptive roots are not deepened and energized in each succeeding generation. To understand what is happening, we must move from the sight of reality to the insight of truth.

Part II

The Insight of Truth

For the word of God is living and active. Sharper than any double-edged sword, it penetrates even to dividing soul and spirit, joints and marrow, it judges the thoughts and attitudes of the heart.

—Hebrews 4:12

He who tells the truth must keep one foot in the stirrup.

—Arabian Proverb

3 The Seeking Generation

 How do Great Awakenings influence our spiritual history? We have already seen how they have a role in writing the history of our American democracy, building a moral consensus, and setting the agenda for social reform. Perhaps, to our surprise, we have also learned that Evangelicals have been instrumental in bringing vision and vitality to our society through their leadership in the Great Awakenings. At the same time, we are saddened to discover that the Evangelical agenda for social reform is frequently co-opted by secular and political interests. When this happens, the biblical roots are cut so that Evangelicals become a counterculture in opposition to those political interests. If there is one lesson to be learned, it is that *Evangelical Christians must renew the vision and vitality for Great Awakenings in each generation.* Elton Trueblood once said that Christians in each generation must "outthink the opposition."[1] An appropriate paraphrase of Trueblood's words is that Evangelical Christians in each generation must "renew the roots" with their own vision and vitality.

What part do Great Awakenings play in shaping our American character, defining our spiritual ideals, and applying our Christian faith to a changing society? Assuming that Robert Fogel is right when he claims that the Fourth Great Awakening is a response to the need for "spiritual equity" so that all people in a diverse society can achieve some form of "self-actualization," the answer to this question begins to unfold.

SHAPING AMERICAN CHARACTER

The drive for self-actualization is not new. In truth, it is the oldest drive in human nature. Adam reveals the distorted drive for self-actualization as the original sin when he succumbs to the temptation to be as wise as God. Throughout human history, the same twisted motivation shows itself in an infinite number of guises. As inheritors of Adam's nature, each of us knows how self-actualization can mask our motives and hide our sins.

None of us, then, will be surprised to learn that the psychological drive for self-actualization as an outcome of the Fourth Great Awakening is evidence of a worthy spiritual motive gone wrong. More surprising is the changing attitude of Evangelical Christians to the theory and methods of behavioral sciences such as psychology, sociology, and economics as resources for truth. Not more than a generation ago, Evangelical Christians were antagonists of the behavioral sciences. Psychology was opposed because of Freudian theory, sociology was denied because of its cultural relativity, and economics was feared because of its socialistic leanings. A generation later, we find that Evangelicals are not only accommodated to these disciplines but also actually accept their theories and methods as guides for the development of mission and ministry.

The Fourth Great Awakening is our case in point. Fogel's conclusion that self-actualization is the spiritual goal for the Fourth Great Awakening comes from a background in which secular prophets have led the way in warning that radical self-interest has become a dominant and pervasive force among us. At the same time, Evangelical Christians are tending to accept self-actualization as a worthy goal for mission and ministry.

INVADING OUR CULTURE

The Psychological Era—1960s and 1970s. Since the 1960s, scholars have been tracing the rising influence of self-interest in American society. Christian readers will immediately think of C. S. Lewis's *The Abolition of Man* and Elton Trueblood's *The Predicament of Modern Man* as classic texts in which the authors foresee the human loss that occurs when relative values replace absolute truth and the roots of our spiritual nature are cut. Later, from a secular perspective, Christopher Lasch wrote *The Culture of Narcissism* in which he identifies the rise of the Radical Self as characteristic of our society and especially the "Me" generation of the 1970s. In *New Rules: Searching for Self-fulFillment in a World Turned Upside Down,* Daniel Yankelovich notes the same characteristic of self-interest dictating both formal and informal human relationships in what he calls "giving/getting" contracts. Gone are the days of personal dedication to an institution or organization with faith, loyalty, and even sacrifice. Yankelovich sees us negotiating our personal and professional relationships by making sure that we "get" as much as we "give." Robert Bellah sharpens these observations in *Habits of the Heart* when he writes that radical individualism has become the dominant influence shaping American character. According to Bellah, "To be what we want to be for our good" and "To do what we want to do for our own pleasure" are the new credos for our behavior.

Paralleling the studies of rising self-interest in the secular scene, Evangelical Christians in the 1960s were opening their arms to psychological theory and therapeutic methods. What was once opposition now passes from accommodation to uncritical acceptance. By the 1970s, counseling psychology is a full partner with the methods of ministry.

My own life history serves as an example. While a seminary student in the 1950s, I became one of the first Evangelicals to enroll in a program for clinical pastoral psychology at the University of Michigan. My decision met opposition from seminary professors who feared that I would become tainted by Freudian theory and nondirective counseling methods. The fear was well founded, but the tainting was limited. When I returned to seminary for my senior year, three different professors were assigned to grill me. With one of them I made the foolish mistake of telling him how I had changed my opinion about Episcopalians. My father used to quip that Episcopalians were just Roman Catholics who flunked Latin. In the clinical experience, however, I had discovered that the Episcopalian seminarians in the clinical program were truer to the faith than I was. After the professor got over his shock and asked me what I meant by those words, I told him how I had begun the clinical experience by submitting to all of the methods of nondirective counseling, even with desperate and dying patients. It was the smoking and drinking Episcopalian seminarians who rebelled first. In direct opposition to the methods of nondirective counseling, they refused to respond to the desperate pleas of dying patients by saying, "Uh, huh. How do you feel about that?" Instead, they put me to shame by quoting Scripture and praying with their patients. Out of that experience, I restudied the theory of personality behind nondirective counseling and discovered its contradictions with biblical faith. Consequently, I reworked my theory of personality and counseling methods from a biblical basis. Later, I wrote *The Jesus Model* as an attempt to integrate psychological theory with biblical revelation through the example of Jesus, the Master Counselor.

In the 1960s, as secular authors were uncovering self-interest in the attitudes of the "Me" generation, Evangelical Christian authors were co-opting the goal of self-actualization in the tenets of relational theology. Keith Miller's book *A Taste of New Wine* might be considered a forerunner for this movement. Bruce Larson added his volume titled *The Relational Revolution* in which he sums up relational theology in the words "to affirm in others what Christ affirms in us." Although both of these men were solid in biblical theology, the shift of emphasis toward relationships in Christian faith had its prompting in psychological theory and counseling methods. Following this theme, Evangelicals enthusiastically embraced Thomas A. Harris's book *I'm OK—You're OK* without discerning its basis in transactional analysis rather than biblical theology. Finding momentum in this literature, scores of seminars combined psychological health with spiritual growth. More often than not, it seemed as if Abraham Maslow's hierarchy of values served as the foundational truth for this movement and biblical theology was used primarily to sanctify the theory. If this observation seems too extreme, Robert Fogel bases his book *The Fourth Great Awakening* upon the premise that the drive for spiritual equity led by Evangelicals is synonymous with the drive for Maslow's goal of self-actualization.

If the relational theology of the 1960s and 1970s has a champion, it has to be Robert Schuller, pastor of the Crystal Cathedral. Taking up where Norman Vincent Peale left off, Schuller built his ministry on the power of positive thinking, and following in the image of Bishop Fulton Sheen, he found his platform on national television. In both his speaking and his writing, Schuller tends to favor the affirmations of psychological language over the hard truth of New Testament terminology. Very seldom are the words "sin," "conviction," "repentance," and "confession" heard in his sermons or read in his books. In their place are such psychological terms as "negative past experience," "low self-esteem," "positive thinking," and "human potential." Schuller's continuing popularity through three decades is evidence that Evangelical Christians not only have made peace with psychological theory but also see it on the leading edge of mission for an age that will no longer accept the hard truth of the gospel. In one way or another, each of us is probably guilty of substituting therapy for theology.

The Sociological Era—1980s and 1990s. Once Evangelicals dropped their opposition to the behavioral sciences, even sociology became an ally. Earlier, sociology was suspect because its studies of cultures were grounded in a relativism that forsook absolutes in moral values. In the 1970s, however, the church growth movement was hailed as the methodology for evangelism in a changing world. No one dared to stop and ask about the premises of cultural anthropology that are based on relative values and find success among "people groups" who are homogeneous, "like" us, and ready for the gospel. Although the movement corrects the old idea of missionary imperialism by the introduction of "contextualization" for world evangelism, it also carries the possible fault of subordinating the gospel to the cultural context.

The social sciences got another boost when George Gallup Jr. published the results of his survey showing evidence of a "born-again movement" in American society. Gallup's poll in 1976 showed that 44 million Americans professed to be "born-again, Bible-believing, and witnessing" Christians. This finding led to *Time* magazine declaring 1976 as "The Year of the Evangelical," followed by Jimmy Carter's election as president of the United States and the Moral Majority's show of muscle in the political arena. Since then, Evangelicals have read sociological polls as if they were divine revelation. George Gallup Jr., a devout Christian, not only discovered the Born-Again Movement but also traced its outcomes in the lives and behaviors of new believers. George Barna, another pollster, caught the high tide of religious surveys and made his reputation with such provocative studies as *The Frog in the Kettle*. Now, cues for vision and vitality are taken from the findings of the Gallup poll and the Barna report so long as they are favorable to the cause. If not, they are either ignored or contested as lacking objectivity.

In the 1990s, the behavioral sciences gained another step toward favor with Evangelical Christians. Interview techniques were joined with the sampling of surveys to become the authoritative way of describing and predicting religious behavior. Through personal interviews, Robert Wuthnow and Wade Clark Roof won their place on the leading edge of this research. Wuthnow's *The Restructuring of American Religion* uses interview techniques to describe the shape of institutional religion, and his *After Heaven: Spirituality in America Since the 1950s* describes the changing character of individual religion. Wade Clark Roof complements these studies with his own longitudinal interviews with individuals. Out of his interviews have come books titled *A Generation of Seekers* followed by *Spiritual Marketplace* (2000). Both Wuthnow and Roof conclude that institutional religion is giving way to individual faith and that the "boomer" generation is on a spiritual quest that may become an end in itself.

The Economic Era—1990s to the Present. Even stranger than fiction, economics has become an ally of Evangelical Christianity in the 21st century. Just a generation ago, conservative Christians condemned economic theory as socialistic. When Adam Smith's "unseen hand" of automatic harmony, the undergirding principle of capitalism, was cited to be the result of competitive self-interest, the critics were condemned as communists. How well I remember speaking at an evangelical think tank in Kansas City. My suggestion that the New Testament model in Acts 2:44 made "all things . . . common" (NASB) raised the hackles of my conservative listeners. Heads vigorously shook "No" as I spoke, and respondents voiced their rebuttal. I was condemned as "liberal" for raising the question and "socialist" for proposing a politically incorrect answer. The right of private property was assumed to be sacrosanct among Christians.

We have succumbed in other areas that are essentially grounded in economic theory. One of those areas is the broad category called "management." Again, my memory serves me well. In 1982, when I was introduced as the new president of Asbury Theological Seminary, I presented the vision of "world Wesleyan leadership" for the future of the institution. The term "leadership" was immediately assailed as elitist and unbiblical. Even after defining the term in an incarnational context with the servanthood of Jesus as our model, the suspicions remained.

How times have changed. Evangelicals no longer apologize for touting "leadership" as a working principle for education and evangelism on the front edge of the movement. Books on leadership have become best-sellers, and centers for leadership have sprung up across the nation. Even the term "servant leadership" is no longer necessary. Boldly and baldly, denominations and parachurch agencies are staking their future on leadership development. How can we account for this radical about-face? Once again, it appears as if Evangelical Christianity is marching to the drumbeat of a behavioral science.

The Management Model

Management theory, with a focus on leadership, has become a top priority in the corporate world. Moving away from the crass economic motive of the bottom line and a cold, scientific approach to organizational behavior, corporations have come to realize that the future depends on developing leaders of quality who can flex with the conflicting demands of an e-world economy. When all is said and done, however, a profit for the shareholders is still the ultimate and legitimate goal of the corporate community. Evangelicals, then, are following the pattern of the past. Just as psychology and sociology have been turned from enemies to allies, leadership theory derived from economic motives is now enthusiastically accepted by Evangelicals. If the pattern of the past holds true, this trend will also pass. Leadership development is a tool that is consistent with Jesus' preparation of His disciples for their ministry after His ascension, but it is not the cure-all and end-all for the future growth and vitality of the Church. When a new trend comes along, leadership development will take a place beside the church growth movement of the 1970s and the church planting movement of the 1980s as a tool but not the total answer.

Running parallel with leadership development in the Evangelical community is the emphasis on marketing the gospel. Both of these ideas are rooted in economic theory. The title of Wade Clark Roof's book, *Spiritual Marketplace,* speaks volumes to us. Evangelicals are adjusting their ministries to the interests of the consumer. Naturally, then, the spiritual environment is described as a "marketplace." The meaning of the word, however, is cause for concern. Transactions in a marketplace are determined by an exchange of values from which the buyer and the seller both benefit. So while "equity" is the goal of a market transaction, self-interest is the motivator for negotiations. Nothing could be farther from Christian redemption. Whatever happened to the sinner's song, "In my hand no price I bring; / Simply to Thy cross I cling"?

The conflict between biblical faith and market spirituality peaks in Fogel's book *The Fourth Great Awakening.* As an economist, he speaks of "spiritual equity" from a marketing point of view, with the goal of "self-actualization" as the bottom line for the transaction. Although he credits Evangelicals for being leaders of Great Awakenings, he does not understand the price that is paid for our redemption. Instead, Fogel sees good in the spiritual cycle when biblical roots are cut and a secular agenda is activated. It takes a Martin Marty to put the spiritual quest into perspective when he announces that he will give a speech under the title "To Market, To Market, To Buy a Bit of Purity."

CHALLENGING OUR FAITH

With spirituality as the question and self-actualization as the goal, our seeking generation has made a major shift in the fundamentals of faith development. As a puzzling mix of Christianity,

Eastern religions, New Age philosophy, and the behavioral sciences, faith development now proceeds on these premises:

- Spirituality is more important than theology.
- Spiritual search is more important than discovery.
- Spiritual exercise is more important than belief.
- Spiritual becoming is more important than being.
- Spiritual insight is more important than behavior.

Because these are dilemmas created out of half-truths, they are especially dangerous. Yet they are part of the reality with which biblical leaders must deal. Thus they cannot be categorically dismissed.

Wesleyans might return to their history to ask, "How would John Wesley respond to these dilemmas?" We remember that he reached out to his changing culture in the 18th century with innovative methods that did not compromise the message of biblical truth or the mission of the Church. When we look at Wesley's way of confronting the culture and challenging the Church, we again see his Spirit-guided genius for leadership. Rather than segmenting the elements of faith development into opposites and pushing them to extremes, such as spirituality versus theology, he found the critical balance between the two and built a supportive system to nurture that balance. The same can be said for the tendency to create conflict between search and discovery, exercise and experience, becoming and being, insight and behavior. In each case, Wesley found the biblical balance for his message, his mission, and his methods. Wesleyan leaders today are faced with the same challenge. Can we bring balance to the extremes of spiritual search that are testing our message, mission, and methods in the 21st century?

4 The Pervasive Self

Self-interest has become a dominant and pervasive force shaping our character and our culture during the decades since the 1960s. Secular observers of the contemporary scene do not shy away from this conclusion. One observer describes the changing scene as a shift in the image of the American character from the "self-made man" to the "man-made self." Horatio Alger personifies the former and Donald Trump idealizes the latter. And the influence of self-interest does not stop with individuals. Corporations and governmental institutions are designing their strategies around the assumptions of radical individualism. Most troubling, however, is the impact of self-interest on our primary institutions—home, church, and school. We understand what Faith Popcorn says when she concludes that "Egonomics" are in overdrive. Like an infective virus on a computer, the Radical Self is rewriting our history and reshaping our society. To secular observers, the final evidence is the fact that individual self-interest is now overriding the "common good." Christians have a special stake in this concern because the common good that has distinguished our society is a product of the biblical vision that Alexis de Tocqueville saw when he described America as a "nation with the soul of a church." So as radical self-interest dominates our character and pervades our institutions, Christians will find themselves engaged in spiritual conflict.

CREATING A SPIRITUAL CONFLICT

Although "self-actualization" is a laudable term for psychological development to a level of maturity, it is based upon premises that contradict the command of Jesus Christ. Three contradictions are evident.

First, *self-actualization implies the inherent goodness of human nature* that only needs to be developed, whereas the gospel assumes that we are born in sin and find redemption only in the grace of Jesus Christ. Evangelical advocates of relational theology may dispute this contention. Some would say that being sensitive to the needs of seekers is the only way in which the gospel can break through to the postmodern mind. By beginning with the needs of self-interest, the opportunity is opened for a follow-up with the harder truth of the gospel. This assumes, of course, that the nurturing process for new believers includes instruction in such realities as conviction for sin, repentance from sin, justification through the blood of Christ, and sanctification by the cleansing and empowering of the Holy Spirit. Such an assumption is contrary to the pattern of preaching in the New Testament that begins with conviction for sin and offers hope only in the cross of Christ.

As a couple who has moved across the country and up the Pacific coast in recent years, my wife and I have attended multiple forms of seeker-sensitive services in megachurches. While many of those in our generation find the music difficult to accept, our distress is found in the sermons. Fifty minutes of speaking can go on without the mentioning of sin, conviction, repentance, the Cross, or even the name of Jesus Christ. Although there is no doubt about the appeal of these messages for thousands of worshipers, if an invitation is given, it is limited to such words as, "Put your hand in the hand of God." For the sake of the relationship, the preaching of the Cross as the price for sin is minimized and the conviction for sin is reduced to a personal need for acceptance. As usual, it appears that we have overcorrected for the hell and brimstone preaching of the past by giving spiritual seekers what they want as their introduction to the gospel. In some cases where new believers are discipled in small groups and engaging in self-giving ministries, there is evidence of spiritual maturity. In too many cases, however, the statistics of growth are kept artificially high by the rate of turnover because attendees do not become converts and converts do not become disciples. Only time will tell whether or not this approach will produce a generation of believers whose spiritual maturity is the result of a biblically grounded faith.

Second, *self-actualization foresees a self-affirming process leading to wholeness*, whereas the gospel commands self-death as the path to holiness. "Whoever wishes to save his life shall lose it; but whoever loses his life for My sake and the gospel's" (Mark 8:35, NASB) is not a welcome word for the proponents of self-actualization. Even the terminology used to describe spiritual maturity reflects the influence of self-actualization. "Holiness" is a disputed word, even among its ad-

vocates in Holiness denominations. "Wholeness" is far more acceptable but also more revealing. Just as the biblical term "grace" is
being redeemed in Evangelical literature, "holiness" needs to be redeemed as well. As we will note later, "holiness" is a term that immediately takes us into the presence of the holy God where we see
ourselves as sinners without hope for justification except through the
blood of Jesus Christ. "Wholeness," however, begins at the opposite
end of the spectrum with ourselves at the center and our own potential as the primary resource. Never the twain shall meet.

Third, and most important, is the fact that *self is at the center of
self-actualization,* whereas Jesus Christ is at the center of the self-
giving life. With self at the center, we begin to understand the deeper meaning of such terms as "self-actualization," "self-fulfillment,"
"self-identification," and "self-interest." With Christ at the center,
however, the terms of "self-giving," "self-sacrifice," and "self-death"
come front and center in our vocabulary. The "man-made self" is a
far cry from the biblical description of the "Christ-made self" that
we find in the promise that "we, who with unveiled faces all reflect
the Lord's glory, are being transformed into his likeness with ever-
increasing glory, which comes from the Lord, who is the Spirit"
(2 Cor. 3:18). Thus if Robert Fogel is correct and "self-actualization"
is the spiritual goal of the Fourth Great Awakening, we can quickly
see its implications for biblical Christianity and the Evangelical
movement. Like dominoes falling one after another, once the domino of "self-actualization" is toppled, the others follow one by one.

TOPPLING THE DOMINOES

The first domino to fall when tipped by self-actualization is
communal faith. Rather than identifying with the Body of Christ,
spiritual seekers whose goal is self-actualization tend toward a privatized faith. This was not a surprise to us back in the 1970s when
Daniel Yankelovich found members of the "Me" generation who
said, "I am my own faith." Today, however, the infectious influence
of self-interest has spread to born-again Christians. Among the millions who profess belief in Jesus Christ, an increasing number hold
their faith as a personal and private experience. We read the Bible
according to our own needs, develop a theology according to our
own perceptions, and pursue a lifestyle not unlike our secular peers.
Martin Marty, the church historian, describes our contemporary
faith as "personal, private, provincial, and parochial."

As the inevitable companion of privatized religion, another domino falls with the loss of *denominational connection.* We should not be surprised that traditional denominations and their incumbent hierarchies are the first to feel the effect of privatized religion. Lyle Schaller cites 27 reasons for the decline of denomination. In many cases, the role of the denomination has been reduced to ministerial credentialing and management of the pension fund.[1] Neither of these is sufficient to preserve denominationalism in the future. For good reason, Wuthnow has used the term "postdenominational" to describe the current status of our traditional religious hierarchies.

In addition to the fact that denominations no longer serve the needs that created them in the first place, any form of hierarchy is considered an obstacle to the drive for self-actualization. The rebellion against authority and the anti-institutional attitudes of the 1960s have become permanent in the minds of the following generations.

Wuthnow sees another factor in the movement away from fellowship through religious institutions. Because of our ever-increasing mobility in the 21st century, he compares a past generation seeking a "spirituality of dwelling" with the new generation's "spirituality of seeking." Even in instances where the new generation of believers seek out relational connections with other members of the Christian family in small support groups, the bonding is usually based on meeting an individual need or interest. The biblical balance (Acts 2:46) of worship in the "great congregation" with fellowship in small groups that are the "church within the church" has been lost.

As the dominoes continue to be toppled by the drive for self-actualization, *theological integrity* is the next to fall. Although the facts are in, Evangelicals do not seem to be alarmed by what Charles Colson calls "salad bar Christianity" in a smorgasbord of truth. Polls of those who profess to be born again show a generation of Christians who are not sure what or why they believe, pick and choose among absolutes, avoid the judgment of falsehood, tolerate evil, and live without significant distinction from their secular peers. Wade Clark Roof, in his book *Spiritual Marketplace,* diagnoses the disease as the cancer of "self-seeking spirituality."

In natural sequence, we are not surprised to learn that another domino falls, because the erosion of theological integrity leads directly to *religious syncretism.* Just at the time when Evangelical Christians are reluctant to confront evil or engage falsehood, religious diversity is fast becoming one the greatest challenges to our faith. To the old mix of Protestants, Catholics, and Jews are now added the multiplying numbers of Muslims, Hindus, and Confucians, all of whom are seeking their place and their power in the land of religious freedom. When Al Gore chose Joseph Lieberman, a modern Orthodox Jew, as his running mate, he sent the signal far and wide that the Democratic party would be the party of tolerance for religious diversity. Without a doubt, this will be one of the greatest challenges to Evangelical faith in the coming years. How can we stay true to the democratic ideal of religious diversity without compromising the absolutes of biblical truth? A generation that is reluctant to impose its views on others has already shown its colors in the evidence that half of all "born-again" baby boomers believe that "if people are good enough, they can earn a place in heaven." Already, one of the most persistent questions asked by Christian teens is whether or not the heathen can be saved. While couching the question in the context of those who have never heard the gospel, they are also thinking about their Asian, African, and Latin friends who are classmates in school. Unless their questions are answered, universalism may be just a short step away for the next generation.

The dominoes continue to fall with the weakening of *moral conviction* among Evangelicals. Earlier, we noted that Evangelicals have a reputation for being vigorous opponents of moral evil yet have come to soften their stance to the point of tolerating the evil. Motion pictures are the classic example of this process. From complete prohibition against movies, Evangelicals are now tolerant of their influence.

I found myself caught in this trap while listening to the car radio one day. A religious station was broadcasting the morning worship of a church where the youth pastor was substituting for the senior pastor as preacher of the day. I almost turned the radio off because the young man was violating most of the principles of homiletics. But then, with my finger on the "Off" button, he drove an arrow of conviction into my soul by mentioning the movies that Christians can now rent and watch at home, including those that are R-rated and we wouldn't go to the theater to see. His next sentence sticks forever in my mind. "Are we now laughing at the things for which Christ died?" The homiletics might have been weak, but the truth was pungent. Moral tolerance in a permissive society is an ever-present danger.

Accompanying this change in our moral outlook is the crash of the domino we know as *aggressive evangelism.* Irony strikes again.

Just when other faiths, sects, and cults are gaining momentum by aggressive evangelism, Evangelical Christians are apologizing for their militancy of the past. Behind the apology, however, is an ominous truth. Once the dominoes of theological integrity, Christian particularism, and moral conviction have fallen, the passion for evangelism wanes. One of the sad findings of contemporary surveys is the fact that a rising percentage of younger Evangelicals feel as if they should not "impose" their convictions upon others. How times have changed. Even in the 1960s, personal evangelism was emphasized for Christian witness. But beginning with the 1970s, the scene shifted toward the techniques of church growth; in the 1980s, church planting had its day; and in 1990s, spiritual marketing was favored as the evangelistic technique. Once again, the terms we use reveal our emphasis. In the 21st century, "lifestyle evangelism" and "contagious Christianity" suggest modifications that are more affirmative and less aggressive than older techniques. If moral tolerance continues to grow and characterize the attitude of Evangelical Christians, we can expect evangelism to lose its passion in a diverse culture and for political desperation to take its place. This is a losing battle because our opponents have learned that a single issue advanced with passion, whether it is gay rights, environmental protection, health care, or world trade, will prevail in the political realm. Unless the gospel is advanced with passion as the single message of Christians, it will pale against the claims and convictions of others.

Self-actualization as a spiritual goal continues to take its toll as the domino of *Christian compassion* falls. Evidence is mounting that Evangelical Christians of the Fourth Great Awakening are not as self-giving for the common good as their earlier counterparts. By turning inward toward self-actualization, the ethic of "disinterested benevolence" suffers. Robert Wuthnow's study of the difference between conservative and liberal Christians confirms this fact. Because liberal Christians still see the hope of redemption through social action, they are active in community causes for relief and justice. Conservative Christians, however, place such emphasis upon individual redemption that they shy away from the liberal taint. But if aggressive evangelism is no longer their strategy, they forfeit their responsibility for both personal and social redemption.

Here is where irony checks in. Out of the same drive for self-actualization, advocates of individual rights lay their claims. Foremost is the issue of abortion. Pro-choice advocates build their case on the woman's right to control her own body and decision for her own interest. Following closely are the issues of feminists and gay activists, whose platforms are geared to individualistic and instrumental values with little reference to the common good other than the catchall of "equal rights." Religious and political conservatives, reacting against these claims, are accused of trying to impose their convictions on others by constitutional amendment and legislative action. This is part of the rebellion against any form of institutional governance that restricts individual rights. Bellah's observations about the tenets that are shaping American character seem to be coming true. "To be what one wants to be for one's own good" and "To do what one wants to do for one's own pleasure" may well represent the extreme of self-actualization.

Finally, *spiritual accountability* joins the long string of fallen dominoes. With the privatization of faith comes the lack of accountability to the Body of Christ. With the loss of denominational connection comes the lack of accountability to corporate discipline. Both of these losses can be brushed aside by the seeker of self-actualization saying, "I am accountable only to God." But this statement is a ruse. Ultimately, when self-interest rules, we are accountable only to ourselves. More than temporal accountability is involved. The larger question is, "How will we stand before God in the final Judgment?" or "What is our view of heaven and hell?" In Evangelical circles, we are seeing a new phase of the debate over the nature of hell. Traditional viewpoints that hold that hell is physical or spiritual torment with eternal separation from God are giving way to conditionalism and univeralism. Conditionalism and its partner, annihilationism, limit eternal punishment of the wicked to a period after which they will be extinct. Universalism, not unknown among Evangelicals, foresees a loving God forgiving even the worst of sinners after a period of punishment. Although these theories of eternal punishment sound like the meanderings of esoteric theologians, they play directly into the hands of spiritual self-seekers who place themselves rather than a holy God at the center of the universe.

GAINING OUR PERSPECTIVE

At first glance, the fall of the dominoes may seem to be another litany of woes pronounced upon a sinful society. Let no one be mistaken. Our culture has been corrupted at the core by radical self-interest. Like an infectious disease that invades the system and works insidiously without apparent symptoms, self-interest has contaminated the depth and breadth of our societal and spiritual life. How, then, do we read these symptoms? Several options are before us. If we are reading the signs of the times from the perspective of a dispensational premillennialist, we see evidence of the last days before the second coming of Christ. Joining them in a prophetic pronouncement from a secular point of view would be William Strauss and Neil Howe, mentioned earlier as the authors of *The Fourth Turning: An American Prophecy.* For them, the symptoms of radical self-interest represent the "unraveling" of our social fabric and predict the inevitable catastrophe required to start a new life cycle.[2] But at the other extreme, if we are in agreement with Robert Fogel, the thirst for "spiritual equity" in a religiously diverse culture is another progressive step toward the democratic ideal.

Time magazine adds another perspective for serious consideration. Under the title "New Lights of the Spirit," the religion editors observed that "America's evangelical community, usually at the national vital and visionary edge, is uncharacteristically subdued as it ponders a retreat from the political activism of the 1980s and 1990s. That leaves the dreaming to the folks on the country's cultural margins or, more specifically, to those intent on sharing the margin's insights with the mainstream." So with Evangelical Christians apparently on the sidelines of "vision and vitality," *Time* finds the new wave of spiritual innovators among African-American Pentecostals, Hispanic Catholics, and Tibetan Buddhists.[3] If so, it is time for Evangelicals to reclaim their role in Joel's vision, "Your old men will dream dreams, your young men will see visions" (2:28).

Joel's prophecy brings us back to a biblical and Wesleyan viewpoint of the spiritual search for self-actualization. Realism requires that we pronounce radical self-interest as both a dominant and pervasive force in our society as evidence of sin in human nature. True to biblical truth, we must be pessimistic about human nature. But as Wesleyans, we are also optimistic about grace. J. B. Phillips rang the bells of hope for us in his translation of Rom. 5:20, "Yet, though sin is wide and deep, thank God, His grace is wider and deeper still!" With full confidence, we can claim with optimism that grace is still at work. Rather than slumping under the evidence that self-interest has become a dominant and pervasive force in our society, confidence in the work of the Holy Spirit leads us to lay claim to the fact that grace is more dominant and more pervasive than any of the counterforces of sin. Here is where we draw the difference between psychological theory and biblical faith. Psychological theory begins with the ideal of human goodness only to be mugged by the reality of human sin. Biblical faith begins with the reality of human sin in order to see the promise of God's grace as the only hope of our redemption. If we must err, let it be on the side of "abounding" grace. Radical self-interest, as expressed in the spiritual quest of a seeking generation, is at one and the same time either the bane or the boon of our spiritual future.

Here is where Wesleyans must take a hard look at our role and responsibility in the 21st century. To what extent is the quest of the Fourth Great Awakening a cry for biblical holiness in the name of spirituality? If so, how can we respond to this thirst with new vision and fresh vitality? The answer is to bring the "optimism of grace" into every phase of our spiritual agenda for the 21st century. Like the apostle Paul standing in the marketplace at Athens and announcing Jesus Christ as the Person whom the Greeks were seeking in their niche "TO AN UNKNOWN GOD" (Acts 17:23), Wesleyan leaders have the opportunity to send the clarion call that the Holy Spirit is the Person whom this generation seeks in its drive for self-actualization. To do this, however, the "optimism of grace" must move us from the insight of truth into the foresight of hope.

A DAY OF INFAMY

If ever we needed the hope of grace, it is now. September 11, 2001, is a day of infamy that is indelibly etched in our national memory. On this day, evil won a round in the cosmic conflict and American history divided once again between "before" and "after." Stopped in our tracks, we cannot go forward into part III—"The Foresight of Hope" without reflecting upon the spiritual implications of that horrendous day. Among the questions that everyone is asking, none is more important than the query, "Was it the end or the beginning of a Great Awakening?"

5 Awakening at Ground Zero

 At precisely 8:47 A.M. on September 11, 2001, a commercial airliner carrying innocent passengers was flung like a Molotov cocktail into the North Tower of the World Trade Center in New York City. While still in shock at seeing the ball of flame rise in the tower, a second airliner smashed into the South Tower. At the same time, a flash of news told of another hijacked plane heading for the White House in Washington, D.C. Changing course at the last minute, it dove directly into the side of the Pentagon.

All of us know exactly where we were when we first heard the news of the terrorist attacks. Like the bombing of Pearl Harbor and the assassination of President John F. Kennedy, this moment when American history was rewritten and the American character was tested is unforgettable. Now in the aftermath of this cataclysmic event, commentators, historians, and pundits are hard at work trying to interpret the meaning of this latest turning point in human history. Eventually, theologians, Church historians, and students of prophecy will no doubt add their perspective to the mix.

Readers of this book also deserve to ask the question, "How do the terrorist attacks of September 11, 2001, relate to the Great Awakenings in American history?" The question is most relevant because we have been contending that American history is written in the cycles of the Great Awakenings. We have also contended that we are living in the mature years of the Fourth Great Awakening, which began in the 1970s. Both the spiritual and secular cycles of that Great Awakening have turned as political strategists have co-opted the redemptive impulse into a political agenda. Consequently, Evangelical Christian leaders are called to confront a culture in which the Radical Self is the dominant and pervasive force shaping our American character. If so, has an act of terrorism brought an end to the Fourth Great Awakening? Or will the trauma of terrorism be the starting point for the Fifth Great Awakening in American history? In either case, how will the events of September 11th affect the agenda of Wesleyan leadership in the days ahead?

Without presuming to have indisputable answers to these questions, we may glean some insights from viewing this turning point in American history through the lens of the Great Awakenings. At the very least, this infamous day is a wake-up call for the nation and the church.

First, *the terrorist acts awakened us to see the unmasked face of evil.* A generation ago, Karl Menninger wrote a landmark book titled *Whatever Happened to Sin?* Even though he wrote from the viewpoint of a secular psychiatrist, Menninger saw evidence that the reality of human sin had gone underground. His unforgettable words still ring loud and clear, "Cry sin; Cry redemption; cry hope."[1] He knew that without the recovery of the awareness of sin, there is no redemption and there is no hope. Menninger's warning comes to fulfillment in the glorification of the Radical Self. The sin of selfishness is exalted as a virtue in seeking for self-actualization. The credos "To be what we want to be" and "To do what we want to do" are nothing more than sin in the guise of self-fulfillment.

Raw evil wears no such mask. Twice in our generation Satan has bared his demonic face. In the blast that brought down the Murrah Federal Building in Oklahoma City and killed 267 innocent people, we first glimpsed the face of terror in domestic form. Now, the surrealistic sight of hijacked airliners crashing as balls of fire into the towers of the World Trade Center in New York City discloses to us the evil of international terrorism. In both of these traumatic events and the ensuing grief, Christian leaders have been slow to call evil by its name. Labeling these acts as the judgment of God or mouthing platitudes about the good that can come from disaster rings hollow. Sooner or later, however, we must face the fact that the act of terrorism is the sin of the Radical Self infused with the hatred of religious fervor. Elie Wiesel, survivor of Auschwitz, sums it up with the question and answer, "Why, then, the mass murder now? A human earthquake, it was caused by people whose faith has been perverted."[2]

Second, *September 11, 2001, is the day of judgment for the Radical Self.* While we have predicted the time when the Radical Self will be repudiated by the weight of its sinfulness, an international act of terror brought it down in one fell swoop. Suddenly, we see ourselves in the mirror of our self-seeking both as individuals and as a nation. With demonic intensity, the terrorist targeted the symbols of our prosperity and our security. To say that they failed is wrong. They drove our struggling economy into recession, confounded our military might, and turned our security into anxious fear. I reject the idea that God authored the attack to bring judgment upon America or to call us to our senses. Nevertheless, if the disaster dethrones the Radical Self as a dominant and pervasive force in shaping our national character, it will be remembered as our wake-up call.

Third, *the terrorist attack has restored our commitment to the common good.* Selfish individualism abolishes the common good. Our culture had gone so far down that track that our homes, schools, and churches had become "arenas of hostility" rather than "nurturing" places for the common good. Yet redemptive renewal in a Great Awakening always brings with it the spirit of disinterested benevolence. September 11, 2001, dramatically restored that spirit. Every day we hear gripping stories of self-sacrifice among the survivors and rescue workers. Americans have poured out their energy and their money to relieve the families of victims. Because of Great Awakenings, no other people have the distinction of being described as "a nation with the soul of a church." If we can build upon a restored sense of the common good, there is new hope.

Fourth, *the trauma of terrorism has caused us to turn to God.* If Great Awakenings begin with a society spinning out of control and a return to dependence upon God, September 11, 2001, may mark a spiritual turning in our history. President Bush has been front and center with his Christian faith, but not to the extent of excluding the faith of others. In the national prayer service held a week after the attacks, history was made when Muslims, Roman Catholics, and Jews shared the platform with Billy Graham. Equally surprising, no one objects when the singing of "God Bless America" becomes the standard for the seventh inning stretch at baseball games, "Amazing Grace" brings tears to all eyes, and a moment of silence opens school days across the nation. Certainly, September 11, 2001, will be a memorial day for the nation and "In God we trust" will have new meaning.

Fifth, *September 11, 2001, is a potential threat to theological integrity and evangelistic fervor.* A sobering fact lingers behind the religious unity and patriotic resolve we experienced in the days following the terrorist attack. Trauma, personal or national, tends to have a life of its own. After the initial shock, disaster has a way of speeding us in the direction we were going before the event took place. Think back to the toppling of the dominoes caused by a push from the Radical Self. One of those falling dominoes was the loss of theological integrity. Due to the influence of the Radical Self, generic evangelicalism and religious syncretism have already made inroads into the minds of Christians in our generation. Now, in the aftermath of September 11th, there is a new threat to biblical faith. Across the nation, all faiths are finding common ground before God and temporarily putting aside their theological differences. We can expect this response in a time of mourning. But what about the future? Will biblical truth give way to a broad-based ecumenical truce under the name of unity or world peace? If this happens, Christianity has the most to lose. Our millennial generation is already questioning the belief that Jesus Christ is our only hope for salvation. Will the call for religious unity further erode this distinctive claim of our faith? What will happen to Christian evangelism? Will a Christian witness to an Arab neighbor or a Muslim friend be interpreted as unpatriotic and discriminatory? As strange as it seems, a violent act of terrorism could become a partner of the Radical Self by weakening the faith of Evangelical Christians and rendering us timid in our witness. The worst possible result of the September 11th attack would be to neutralize biblical revelation under the banner of "spiritual equity" as a new form of civic religion.

Sixth, *the terrorist attacks awakened us to our kinship in the human family and our partnership in world suffering.* Despite all of the talk about the world becoming a "global village," Americans have basked in the comfort of our geographical security and our economic superiority. Although the media brings the world to our doorstep, we refuse to think of ourselves as members of the human family, not even in the common experience of death itself. The same media shows us graphic pictures of human suffering, but research studies show that we soon suffer from "compassion fatigue" because we do not know the world's suffering firsthand. Now we do. The terrorist attack, heinous as it was, transported us to the streets of Jerusalem, the caves of Afghanistan, the subways of Japan, the killing fields of Columbia, and the villages of the Congo. Their fear is now our fear, their risk is now our risk, and their suffering is now our suffering.

President Bush has tried to lead us back to "normal" by his personal presence at public events. As noble as his gestures have been, we will never return to the "old normal" of the days prior to the September attack. Instead, survivors of the New York City attacks talk about the "new normal" days in which we will live. Every time we go through a security check at the airport, spot a trace of white powder on an envelope, or turn to September on our calendars, we will revisit our memories and relive our fears. Not long ago, an international visitor was asked, "What is the difference between Americans and the rest of the world?" She answered, "Americans do not walk with fear." Now we do. Whether it is American diplomacy, international business, or Christian mission, terrorism has been a breach birth into the human family and into a world of suffering.

Seventh, *we are awakened to the need for national repentance.* Great Awakenings are stimulated by events that expose the raw nature of human sin and the common nature of human guilt. Catastrophes, however, tend to have a cycle of their own. After the assassination of John F. Kennedy, for example, psychiatrists said the American psyche was badly bent and almost broken. Reality shattered our security and revealed that "it can happen here." While adjusting to that shock, the Vietnam War, campus protests, Woodstock, the assassinations of Martin Luther King Jr. and Robert Kennedy, and the killings at Kent State unraveled the fabric of the nation. We were shocked and we were angry, but we did not repent. It took the betrayal of Richard Nixon to bring us to our knees. In the mirror of his lies, we saw the sin in ourselves. As we have seen in tracing the cycle of the fourth Great Awakening, the national malaise in 1974 had a direct connection with the Born-Again Movement of 1976.

If we apply that same perspective to the happenings of September 11, 2001, we are once again victims of traumatic shock to the American psyche. True, it has restored the virtue of the common good under the banner of "God Bless America." True, arrogance has given way to anxiety. True, the stories of self-sacrifice have exposed the fallacy of the Radical Self. True, it has brought us before God in a national service of mourning with leaders of every faith hearing the singing of Amazing Grace. True, it has filled our churches with worshipers who have turned and returned to God. But has it produced the repentance that either refuels or ignites a Great Awakening? Initially, we must say no. The nation appears to be going through the cycle of grief more than the cycle of awakening. Consistent with the "death and dying" cycle of Kübler-Ross, we have witnessed the *denial* of "It can't happen here." Quite naturally, we have seen the *anger* that calls for revenge and the *bargaining* that precedes *acceptance* of the new reality. Whether or not this cycle leads to repentance is still an open question. So far, the calls for mourning are clear and the words of hope are comforting. But has our character shaped by the Radical Self been changed?

I liken the situation to my experience as a chaplain in the surgery ward of the University of Michigan hospital. A standing rule among the chaplains was that almost any surgery patient could be converted on the second day after surgery. On the first day after surgery, patients are numb. On the second day, the medication wears off, the pain arrives, and they are convinced they are going to die. On the third day, however, the mystery of the human body takes over to begin the process of healing. Miraculously, the death wish gives way to the will to live. Body, mind, and soul get a boost that cancels out the memory of a deathbed repentance. In the same way, we will not know the long-term, spiritual impact of September 11, 2001, until we see whether or not national repentance follows national disaster. In a very real sense, this is a defining moment for the Church as well for the nation. With the terrorist bombings, we have met the depths of human evil face-to-face. Will we see that same distorted passion within ourselves, or is it so grotesque it gives us an excuse to say that we are not so bad after all? If the events of September 11, 2001, lead to national repentance as well as a renewal of national unity, we will be a people open to the outpouring of the Spirit. If not, this opportune moment will pass and we will lapse back into the character of the Radical Self, falling victim to the terrorist tactic of Satan. Convinced that we are on the side of the good against the forces of evil, self-interest will reappear in the guise of self-righteousness. I am quick to agree with Charles Colson, who wrote in the November 12, 2001, issue of *Christianity Today*,

> So, yes keep those flags waving and comfort those who mourn, but don't stop there. While we cannot know God's great purposes in these tumultuous and terrifying events, we should be seeking His mercy through, in the full Greek sense of *metanoia:* a changing of our hearts and ways.[3]

Wesleyan leaders must be in the forefront of waving flags and comforting those who mourn. We must also repudiate the Radical Self and urge the return to dependence upon the holy God. But then, we must call the Church and the nation to repentance. During times of panic, people expect their leaders to hold their course. In our case, the "binding address" of biblical holiness in its personal and social dimensions still defines our agenda for Wesleyan leadership.

Whether the events of September 11, 2001, break the spiritual cycle of the past or start the cycle of the Fifth Great Awakening, only time will tell. For us, the charge is clear. Whether confronting the culture or challenging the Church, we must stay our course with the biblical message of wholeness and hope.

Part III

The Foresight of Hope

Praise be to the God and Father of our Lord Jesus Christ!
In his great mercy he has given us new birth into a living
Hope through the resurrection of Jesus Christ from the
dead.

—1 Peter 1:3

Keep your forks. the best is yet to come.

—A Family Tale

6 The Truth of the Holy God

 The issues have now been drawn. Through the sight of reality and the insight of truth, we see the 21st-century challenge to biblical faith and Evangelical Christianity.

- Radical self-interest is a dominant and pervasive force shaping our American character.
- Spirituality defines the search for meaning and wholeness in American life.
- "Self-actualization," a psychological term implying meaning and wholeness, is the personal goal of the search for spirituality in American culture.
- Spiritual equity, defined as self-actualization for all people without the need for the redemptive resources of biblical faith, is the social goal of the Fourth Great Awakening.
- September 11, 2001, a turning point in American history, is a spiritual awakening with both threat and promise.
- Christian leaders, in troubled times, are expected to hold their course for biblical faith and witness.

If these insights are correct, 21st-century Christians are once again in pitched battle against "principalities and powers." The battle is as old as the Garden of Eden and the adversaries are well known. The Radical Self is contending against the holy God in a climate of fear.

Are we ready for this life-and-death struggle? As Shakespeare reminds us, two stars cannot move in the same orbit without catastrophe. The Radical Self and the holy God are on a collision course. Those who hope for a "fender bender" are in for a shock. One or the other of these contending forces will be a total wreck. Of course, those of us who believe in the holy God know the final outcome of the battle. But for our generation, Joshua's cry is still heard, "Choose . . . this day whom you will serve" (Josh. 24:15). If we, as Christian leaders, are faithful to our generation, we will step into the fray and contend for the truth of the holy God. Wesleyan leaders, in particular, cannot sidestep their responsibility. As the message of biblical holiness confronts the culture, it also challenges the Church. The challenge begins with the whole truth of the holy God.

THE HARD TRUTH OF THE HOLY GOD

After our oldest son graduated from a Christian university and enrolled in a secular graduate school for doctoral study, he said he was ready for the question, "Why do you believe in God?" Instead, to his surprise, his professors and peers were asking, "Why do I need God?"

In that unexpected question, we see Swinburne's poetic dream come true, "Glory to Man in the highest! for Man is the master of things." Self, in all of its attributes of self-interest, self-reliance, and self-actualization, has been escalated to the position of God himself. As Robert Bellah and other scholars have noted, radical self-interest is the dominant and pervasive force shaping our American character. Once again, Bible truth is on the scaffold and Christians must make a choice between the secular doctrine of the Radical Self and the biblical doctrine of the holy God.

More than 40 years ago, A. W. Tozer wrote, in the preface to *The Knowledge of the Holy,* "The Church has surrendered her once lofty concept of God and substituted for it one so low, so ignoble, as to be utterly unworthy of thinking, worshiping men. This she has not done deliberately, but little by little and without her knowledge; and her very unawares only makes her situation all the more tragic."[1] Later, in 1973, he was joined by James I. Packer, who gave the reason for writing the classic work *Knowing God:* "Ignorance of God —ignorance both of His ways and the practice of communion with Him—lies at the root of much of the church's weakness today" (preface, 12).[2] Another classic based on the same theme was published 10 years later when J. B. Phillips put his indictment of the Church into his title *Your God Is Too Small.* Skip forward, then, into the 21st century when Donald Bloesch asks the question, "Whatever Happened to God?" in an article in *Christianity Today* and answers: "Evangelical Protestantism is in trouble today as an increasing number of business and professional people are searching for a new church. The complaint I hear most often is that people can no longer sense the sacred either in the preaching or in the liturgy. . . . *What is missing is the fear of God, the experience of God as the Wholly Other*" (emphasis mine).[3]

Based upon these observations from our most esteemed Evangelical Christian leaders, what would A. W. Tozer say about the Church today? Would he repeat his observation that "the low view of God entertained almost universally among Christians is the cause of a hundred lesser evils everywhere among us"?[4] Would he note our dramatic gains in popularity, power, and prosperity only to conclude, "But the alarming thing is that our gains are mostly external and our losses are wholly internal; and since it is the *quality* of our religion that is affected by internal conditions, it may be that *our supposed gains are but losses spread over a wider field*" (emphasis mine)?[5]

As the keynoter for a national conference, I chose the title "The Harder Side of Holiness." The idea came from the television commercial advertising "the softer side of Sears." In the ad, Sears hoped to counter the image of Sears as primarily a seller of hardware and tools. "The softer side of Sears" features clothing, particularly women's clothing, promoted by one of the Charlie's Angels.

Holiness is a biblical truth that also has its "harder" and "softer" side. In our generation, the "softer" side is the popular image in the public mind. Led by the charismatic movement, the emphasis is upon the experiential, ecstatic, and personalized side of holiness. Now, we are also seeing the soft underbelly of "generic holiness" in the search for spirituality in both religious and secular literature. A quick scan of best-selling books in the secular market shows everything from Thomas Merton's *Seven Storey Mountain* to *Chicken Soup for the Soul*. These books indicate a thirst for holiness that usually results in an amalgam of Christianity, Judaism, Buddhism, and New Age philosophy that is essentially free-floating and self-serving.

Among Christian books, spirituality also leads the way, but as a correction for the secular market. Dallas Willard's *The Spirit of the Disciplines* was endorsed by Richard Foster as the "book of the decade" at the end of the 20th century. Foster's own book, *The Celebration of Discipline,* has already been declared a classic in the company of such giants as Thomas à Kempis's *Imitation of Christ* and Blaise Pascal's *Pensees*. Add to these volumes Oswald Chamber's *My Utmost for His Highest* with its special emphasis on personal holiness. The popularity of these books among Christians shows how the thirst for holiness is synonymous with the search for spirituality.

There is no antidote for the ills of the Church other than a return to the hard truth of the holy God. In the contest with the Radical Self, there can be no compromise. Death to the Radical Self is the only alternative. Whether the image is Moses being blinded by the light of God's purity, Isaiah crying "Woe is me" in the presence of His power, or Saul being knocked from his horse by the sight of the Christ, the Radical Self must die and the holy God must reign. At whatever cost, 21st-century Christian leaders must give this message its certain sound. Beginning with our own self-death, we must be bold to preach the hard truth of the holy God.

THE WHOLE TRUTH OF THE HOLY GOD

As the hard truth of the holy God is the corrective for error, the whole truth of the holy God is our affirmation for hope. Once we have bowed before His holy presence, confessed our sin, and cried for repentance, God responds with the healing of His holiness. Wholeness is His promise, not just for what we believe but also for what we are and how we behave.

The holiness of God is the beginning of our salvation. A. W. Tozer wrote, "He is the absolute quintessence of moral excellence, infinitely perfect in righteousness, purity, rectitude, and incomprehensible holiness."[6] No wonder Isaiah fell on his face and cried, "Woe is me! for I am undone" (Isa. 6:5, KJV). In the awe-filled presence of the holy God, we confess our unworthiness and repent of our sins. But our cry is futile except for our understanding that the holy God is more than a dreadful mystery or a wrathful character. He is a personality with an infinite love that leads to the sacrifice of His only Son in the Incarnation, Crucifixion, and Resurrection so that His creation can be redeemed and made holy. If, therefore, our worship is without awe, our experience is without repentance, our preaching is without the Cross, and our practice is without moral excellence and social compassion, it is because we have downsized the character of God and downplayed His holiness.

Reaching into history once again, in 1937 H. Richard Niebuhr stung the conscience of his theological and pastoral colleagues for teaching and preaching that "a God without wrath brought men without sin into a kingdom without judgment through the ministration of a Christ without a Cross."[7] Niebuhr dared to bring this indictment against liberal Christianity in his day. Beginning with a loss of the wrath of a holy God, once again the doctrinal dominoes fall—the sinfulness of humankind, the judgment of the Kingdom, and the Christ without a Cross. Can the same indictment be brought against Evangelical Christianity today? Our theology, our worship, our preaching, our experience, and our practice will give us the answer and set our agenda for the future.

21ST-CENTURY LEADERSHIP INITIATIVES

Once we establish a sound, biblical view of the holiness of God, our responsibility as Wesleyan leaders follows naturally.

1. **We must be lifelong learners in the knowledge of the holy God.** To read a book, take a course, or earn a degree in theology is not enough. Because the nature of God is at the target of continuing attacks from seen and unseen forces, we must go back to biblical basics on a regular schedule. Wesleyan leaders need to begin with a steady diet of reading and rereading the classics of Wesleyan theology, including these: *A Plain Account of Christian Perfection* by John Wesley; *Wesley's Sermons* (vols. 1 and 2) by Albert Outler; *Five Views of Sanctification* by Melvin Dieter; *Wesley and the People Called Methodists* by Richard Heitzenrater; *The Scripture Way of Salvation* by Kenneth Collins; *Exploring Christian Holiness* (vol. 2) by Paul Bassett and William Greathouse; *A Theology of Love* by Mildred Bangs Wynkoop; and A. B. Simpson's *Wholly Sanctified*. Perspective can be added by reading A. W. Tozer's *The Knowledge of the Holy,* James I. Packer's *Knowing God* and *Rediscovering Holiness,* Billy Graham's *The Holy Spirit,* R. C. Sproul's *The Holiness of God,* and Jerry Bridges's *The Pursuit of Holiness.*

An enriching experience awaits us. The goal of our study is to keep fresh in our minds the incomparable image of the holy God, correct theological errors, affirm the wholeness of truth, and claim the promise of the Holy Spirit.

2. **We must take the lead in the worship of the holy God.** It is a false notion that we come to corporate worship to invoke the presence of the holy God. Worship is a total life experience for pastor and people. Rather than assuming that the Spirit of God will break into our corporate worship services, we need the heart preparation of private worship before we come together as a community of faith. Leaders, in particular, must bring the spirit of worship with them. The sense of holy awe, the spirit of confession for our shortcomings, the testimony of His healing, and the expectancy of His continuing presence should characterize our preparation for worship as well as our worship itself. Pastors who ask members of a congregation to be bound together in prayer throughout the time of the worship service are taking seriously their obligation to be leaders of worship. If all of the members of the congregation had their turn in this special assignment, a praying congregation would be the result.

3. **We must lead in the confession of sin and the regularity of**

repentance. Whenever we enter in to the presence of the holy God, we see the reality of our sin and shortcomings. In those moments, confession is not a show of weakness and repentance is not a sign of backsliding. As the saints of the ages make confession and repentance a regular part of their spiritual discipline, we, too, must recover this reality. Part of the fault may rest with the misunderstanding of "perfectionism" in Wesleyan-Holiness history or an equal misunderstanding of "eternal security" in the Calvinist tradition. But the greater fault rests with the deficiency in understanding the holiness of God because of the subtle intrusion of the Radical Self into the theological equation. Confession is too humbling and repentance is too negative for the exaltation of self-interest. It is far easier to affirm our potential than it is to confess our sins and far easier to go forward rather than turn around and start over. As leaders, we must recover the meaning of confession and restore the regularity of repentance in our spiritual journey. Until we take this lead, spiritual growth, for us and our people, will be lopsided in favor of the affirmative self rather than the holiness of God.

Unequivocal truth comes back to us again. The more we grow in the likeness of Jesus Christ, the greater is our thirst for the holiness of God. The ultimate test for pastor and people is a deep hunger for God that can be observed by all who come in contact with us.

4. We must be loving critics of our Evangelical subculture. Prophetic voices are still not welcome among us. Of course, we applaud those who thrash the secular culture and its symptoms of self-interest, but we cast a wary eye at those who dare to diagnose the same symptoms in the Evangelical Christian subculture. When one of our most respected of Evangelical theologians voiced his concern about the diminished concept of God and its consequences in our worship, preaching, and compassion, he was dismissed as a theological throwback and a hidebound traditionalist. "Who can argue with success?" seems to have replaced "Is it true to the Word of God?" as the leading question for assessing our Evangelical subculture. Without becoming doomsayers who see no hope for the Church, we do need to point out areas of our faith and witness that have been contaminated by the infectious spirit of self-interest among us. Any attitudes and action that elevate self at the expense of the holy God must elicit a call for repentance and reform.

5. We must be tough-minded monitors of our motives and methods for ministry. Evangelicals may not want to admit it, but the world is very much with us. As we have seen in the overview of Great Awakenings, Evangelicals have played a major role in shaping our American history and character. Whether we admit it or not, American history and character have also been instrumental in shaping the history and character of Evangelical Christianity. This fact is most evident in the methods of ministry during the last half of the 20th century and into the opening years of the 21st century. Once Evangelicals declared a truce with the social sciences and became enamored with their findings, our methods of ministry have mirrored those findings. Psychology, psychotherapy, sociology, cultural anthropology, management, marketing, and economics are now bedfellows with our ministry, especially evangelism. Certainly these disciplines have much to teach us. But without biblical discernment in adopting their methods, we also buy into their theory, which may counter the very truth we want to proclaim. Because marketing as the front edge of our witness is currently in vogue, it illustrates the point. Marketing theory is based on the premise that the exchange of values between a buyer and a seller results in mutual benefit for each. Psychologists call this exchange "equity theory." To market an automobile, for instance, a dealer must convince a customer that the value of the automobile to be purchased is worth the dollars invested. Self-interest is the underlying motive for the transaction. If the same approach to evangelism is to convince that the Christ has value to bring to the sinner and the sinner has value to bring to the gospel, God is diminished and the truth is compromised.

Marketing the gospel illustrates the fact that we have started on the wrong side of the equation for assessing the methods of ministry. Rather than adopting the methods of the social sciences and letting the fallout influence our concept of the holiness of God, we should start with the holiness of God to critique the methods of evangelism adopted from the social sciences. If we do, most of these methods will be reduced to "techniques" and the panaceas they promise will be seen as "Band-Aids."

6. **Finally, we must be contenders for the whole truth of the holy God.** As we have seen, there are many pretenders to the throne of holiness in the name of spirituality. Some are secular heresies that are easily identified; others are Evangelical in name but piecemeal in truth. Like the "seed-pickers" of truth that Paul identified among the Greeks in Athens, we cannot erect a pantheon of separate niches for belief, being, and behavior based on our image of God or our

theological framework. If we do, we must also create a niche for the "UNKNOWN GOD." As is often said, "He will be God of all, or He will not be God at all."

OH, TO BE WORTHY

The weighty words that prompted A. W. Tozer to write *The Knowledge of the Holy* come to mind:

> The heaviest obligation lying upon the Christian Church today is to purify and elevate her concept of God until it is once more worthy of Him—and of her. In all her prayers and labors this should have first place. We do the greatest service to the next generation of Christians by passing on to them undimmed and undiminished that noble concept of God which we have received from our Hebrew and Christian fathers of generations past.[8]

Biblical leaders of the 21st century will pay heed to those words and breathe the same prayer that Tozer prayed at the end of his writing: "We are left for a season among men, let us faithfully represent Him here."[9]

7 The Experience of a Holy Heart

 Senator Mark Hatfield describes his role as a Christian in politics with this principle: *You can compromise on timing, wording, and procedure but never on principle.* He exemplified that approach throughout his political career, often making both sides mad but never losing the respect of either.

The same working principle has value for us as we consider the experience of the holy heart, a subject that often produces more heat than light among Evangelical Christian leaders. Our starting point is the fact that any Bible-believing Christian acknowledges God's command, Christ's promise, and the Holy Spirit's evidence that we are to be holy. This is the principle that can never be compromised and upon which we all agree. But when it comes to timing, wording, and procedure, controversy flares. Is our heart made holy at the time of conversion, at some subsequent sanctifying moment, or at the time of death? What is the difference between the terms "sanctification" and the "Spirit-filled life"? Are we made holy by the procedure of gradual growth or by a second work of grace? When the answers to these questions are elevated to doctrines without compromise, it is the biblical truth of holiness that suffers.

The time has come to sheath our swords. We dare not fight intramural theological battles at a time of widespread search for spirituality among the general public and a specific desire for personal wholeness among believers. We must begin with the principles upon which we agree. James I. Packer, in his book *Keep in Step with the Spirit,* listed seven principles about biblical holiness that give us a starting point.[1]

1. The nature of holiness is transformation through consecration.
2. The context of holiness is justification through Jesus Christ.

3. The root of holiness is co-crucifixion and co-resurrection with Jesus Christ.
4. The agent of holiness is the Holy Spirit.
5. The experience of holiness is one of conflict.
6. The rule of holiness is God's revealed law.
7. The heart of holiness is the spirit of love.

What would Wesleyan theologians add, subtract, or modify among these principles? Are the differences a matter of timing, wording, and procedure, or are fundamental principles involved? Theological traditions that find their identity in timing, wording, or procedure may find acceptance of these principles a compromise of principle. On the other hand, we dare not gloss over fundamental differences in theology. Wesleyans and Calvinists would certainly separate over the interpretation of the statement "The experience of holiness is one of conflict." Calvinists see the conflict as a continuing struggle with indwelling sin, while Wesleyans see the conflict as growing in the perfection of love against external forces that are constantly vying for the human soul. Within our own ranks of Wesleyans, acceptance might tag us as traitors of the tradition. If so, I only ask for a hearing because my motive is to advance the cause of a biblical truth in which I believe with deep conviction.

A holy heart is both an event and an experience. As a person brought up in the Wesleyan tradition that identifies holiness as the "second work of grace subsequent to justification," I know that timing, wording, and procedure can instantly provoke controversy. Calvinist and Reform theologians, in particular, categorically deny this approach to holiness as a biblically based principle. But when they do, they encounter three dilemmas. First, they have to do a soft-shoe dance around the public event of Pentecost and the personal question of the disciples to new converts, "Have ye received the Holy [Spirit] since ye believed?" (Acts 19:2, KJV).

The second dilemma is to give the experience of biblical holiness the clarion call of a certain trumpet sound. As options to a second work of grace subsequent to justification, our contenders speak of growing into holiness by obedience, define the experience in relational terms, and usually stop short of the wholeness and the fullness that the biblical term specifies. Of course, there is truth in what they say, but after reading their writings on the subject, the desire is awakened, but the promise is unfulfilled.

The third dilemma is deepest and most puzzling. While either

denying or discounting holiness as a spiritual event in the life of believers, their leaders give witness to the experience.

Billy Graham, in the biography titled *The Evangelist,* testifies
that at the age of 28, he sensed the lack of power in his preaching.
While holding an evangelistic meeting in the Welsh town of Gor-
seinon, he met Stephen Olford, a Welsh evangelist who had experienced the fullness of the Holy Spirit under the influence of the Kes-
wick movement in Great Britain. Olford led Graham through a Bible
study related to the "power that comes into the life of the believer
who is willing to submit moment by moment to the sovereignty of
Christ and the authority of the Word."[2] In prayer, then, Graham cried
out with Jacob's prayer, "[Lord,] I will not let thee go, except thou
bless me" (Gen. 32:26, KJV). God answered so decisively that Billy
burst out in testimony, "My heart is so a flood with the Holy Spirit, I
want to laugh and praise God all at the same time."[3] Arising from
prayer, Billy Graham spoke again, "I have it. I am filled. . . . This is
a turning point in my life."[4]

Looking back upon that experience in later years, Graham is
even more specific when he describes that day as "the definitive turning point in his ministry of evangelism."[5] Yet according to his biogra-
pher, Graham is reluctant to make the experience of being filled with
the Spirit as a normative event in the life of the believer. While contending that there are no exceptions to God's command that Christians are to be filled with the Spirit to live a holy life, he distances
himself from the idea of a "second blessing." Instead, he emphasizes
the continuous work of the Holy Spirit in the life of the believer.

Charles Colson, in his autobiography *Born Again* and under the
chapter titled "Unexpected Gift," writes of a turning point in his spiritual development after justification in which the Spirit of God lays
claim to the wholeness of his heart. During a series of Monday evening Bible studies while Colson was in prison, he encounters Jesus'
promise to His disciples, "But when the Holy Spirit has come upon
you, you will receive power" (Acts 1:8, TLB). In response he writes, "It
suddenly occurred to me that I had not asked the Holy Spirit to fill me
with power." A fortnight later, in the same Bible study, the leader pre-
sents the challenge, "Ask for it . . . and the Holy Spirit can take total
control of your life. He will take charge if you open yourselves and
seek—like a personal relationship with Christ, but something far deeper than the mere acknowledgment of God." Once again, Colson responds, "Father, please fill me with your Spirit. Fill me so full there's

room for nothing else, no hatred, no hurt, no bitterness, no exhaustion. Lift me above it all, Father." God answers his prayer with "the most curious effervescent sensation rushing through my body." The next morning Colson writes in his diary, "It was almost like a conversion again—the black cloud passed; it was an incredible experience to have my spirit washed clean."

A paragraph later, Colson acknowledges the ability of the Holy Spirit to work dramatically in us as He did in his life but then qualifies his words with a statement that is more palatable to his Reformed mentors: "More often, I surmise, the Holy Spirit resides in us as a great source of new power, but He serves more as a Helper while we develop our spiritual disciplines."[6]

The contradiction is obvious. Is Charles Colson favored among believers by a personal visitation of the Holy Spirit? Of course not. Charles would be the first to repudiate such a conclusion. But on the other hand, why not admit that the beauty of that event described as a "spirit washed clean" is a present possibility for every believer?

The most unusual testimony, however, comes from R. C. Sproul, one of the most ardent of Reform theologians and also one of the most vocal in his opposition to the Wesleyan-Holiness position. Sproul opens his book *The Holiness of God* with the personal testimony of his continuing spiritual search after his conversion. During a class in philosophy, he confronts the reality of the holy God in the creation story. That night Sproul is awakened with a sense of the "holy." Led out-of-doors to the darkened college chapel, he writes, "I knelt there quietly, allowing the sense of the presence of a holy God to fill me. . . . That moment was life transforming. Something deep in my spirit was settled once for all. From this moment there could no turning back; there could be no erasure of the indelible imprint of its power. I was alone with God. A holy God. An awesome God . . . I knew in that hour that I had tasted of the Holy Grail."[7]

Later, in explaining the experience, he confesses that "something was missing from my early Christian life."[8] Then he chooses the telltale words, "My experience in the classroom, thinking about the creation of the world, was like being born again a second time. It was like being converted, not merely to God the Son, but to God the Father. Suddenly, I had a passion to know God the Father. I wanted to know Him in His majesty, to know Him in His power, to know Him in His august holiness."[9]

While R. C. Sproul might disclaim any connection between his experience and what is called a "second work of grace," the point is made. Holiness, however defined by the nuances of timing, wording, and procedure, is a biblical truth that all Evangelical Christians embrace. Ironically, the testimonies of Billy Graham, Charles Colson, and R. C. Sproul come closer to the description of a "second work of grace" than the experience of John Wesley himself.

On the other side of the ledger, Wesleyans have been guilty of standardizing the event of being filled with the Spirit and neglecting the experience of growing in the fullness of the Spirit. Because of this overbalance, we bring upon ourselves the criticism that we emphasize "sinless perfection" based upon an ecstatic experience that is also a litmus test for our spiritual maturity. While Calvinists lack clarity about the event, Wesleyans lack clarity about the experience. Rather than counting the number of angels that can dance together on the head of a theological pin, both traditions must give first priority to a generation of believers who are thirsting for the fullness of God and needing to give the witness of a holy heart. In other words, we need to come together on the biblical balance that holiness is, by definition, a holistic doctrine.

The Wholeness of Holiness. A holistic doctrine of holiness involves belief and being, command and promise, event and experience, dynamic and discipline. Moreover, it is affirmative rather than negative, dynamic rather than static, and continuous rather than crisis oriented. In sum, it is a model of growth toward spiritual maturity for every believer. According to this model, holiness is

1. *Incipient in our justification.* Basically, there is no debate about the essential role of the Holy Spirit in our justification. He is the Agent of grace who justifies us before the Father and redeems us through His Son. Moreover, when we are justified, we receive the Holy Spirit as our Teacher and our Guide. Whether or not we also receive the fullness of the Spirit at that time of conversion is a matter of debate. But who would deny that we are "babes in Christ" at the time of our conversion? Spiritual maturity is not an instant event. At best, our justification starts us on the road to holiness with the Holy Spirit as our Guide and the promise of His fullness as our destination.

2. *Potential in our formation.* Like a crescendo marked dolce in music, the promise of the Holy Spirit rises with joy in the life of the believer. By cultivating the spiritual disciplines of

prayer, obedience, submission, and repentance, the thirst for the fullness of God deepens in the heart of the new Christian. With that thirst, the dilemma deepens. The struggle of soul is between self-will and the will of God. Although the confrontational issue is highly individualized, the final question is always, "Who shall be my Lord and Master? The Radical Self or the Risen Lord?" As the confrontation escalates, a crisis looms. The conflict, however, is constructive. Before justification, our conflict was rebellion against God. Now, as the Holy Spirit is leading us step-by-step on the path of obedience and submission, our struggle comes from the deepening desire to know the fullness of God. Like the apostle Paul, we want to do that which is good, but find another principle working in us (see Rom. 7). The conflict disturbs our peace, denies our wholeness, and robs us of our power. Echoing the prayer of Jacob with Billy Graham, we cry to God, "I will not let you go until you bless me."

3. *Actual in our sanctification.* Our struggle ends when we realize that the fullness of the Holy Spirit is a gift of grace that God is anxious to give, not a legalistic demand with which He browbeats us. It is also a natural step in our spiritual journey. The timing, therefore, is highly individualized. Our progress toward spiritual maturity may be fast or slow, but the gift of the Holy Spirit is not given until we are ready. It is wrong to expect that sanctification will fill in the gaps in our spiritual growth. If we are standing still or going backward, we are not ready to receive the gift of the Holy Spirit. The gift is ours when we are leaning forward by obedience, longing for all that God has to give us, and waiting in His presence.

As the timing for our sanctification is individualized, so is the point of entry through which the Spirit of God enters our soul. For many, the point of entry is through the will; for others, it is through the emotions; and for still others, it is through the intellect. Wherever the vestiges of the Radical Self remain, the Holy Spirit is the cleansing Agent. For every good reason, the event can still be described as "death to self." Without the crucifixion of self, there is no resurrection with Christ. So whatever the point of entry, the result is the same. The Holy Spirit fills the heart with the perfection of love, leaving no room for any other motive. Although the fullness of the Spirit is not an instant jump to spiritual maturity or the end of spiritual growth, it is, as Billy Graham testified, "the turning point" in our spiritual journey. The course is now set for the walk ahead.

4. *Progressive in our maturation.* Contrary to some expectations, the gift of the Holy Spirit is not the sign and seal of our spiritual maturity. It is a major error to build a formula for the experience based on timing, wording, and procedure. It is equally wrong to give the experience the status of a litmus test for spirituality. Rather, our premise and our promise must be that as we grow *into* holiness, we also grow *in* holiness. Spiritual growth never stops for the soul seeking more of God, and spiritual maturity is never complete for the believer this side of eternity. That is the beauty of the paradox between being filled with the Spirit and being perfected in Christ. When we are sanctified, we are empowered to grow more and more toward perfection in the likeness of His image. True to the nature of growth itself, our steps will still be uneven, repentance will still be required, and Satan will not stop vying for our soul. But the difference is the turning point. Once we have died to self, risen in Christ, and been filled with the Holy Spirit, our attitudes and actions are motivated by love. Any counter motive of self is instantly checked by the Holy Spirit, and His conviction drives us to our knees. In other words, we are growing from a holy heart rather than a conflicted self.

   Most important of all is the evidence of holiness in the gifts of the Spirit. As we mature, we grow in these gifts. The thirst for God is deeper than ever, and the sensitivity to the checks of the Spirit is keener than ever. Here is where Wesleyans part company with Calvinists. The question is whether or not the filling of the Holy Spirit cleanses the believer from the power of indwelling sin. Wesleyans say yes, and Calvinists say no. Consequently, Wesleyans have to explain how indwelling sin is removed and Calvinists have to explain how the fullness of the Spirit can dwell in the heart of the believer and still leave room for the sinful nature.

5. *Perfect in our glorification.* Growth toward spiritual maturity continues throughout our lifetime. Another paradox confronts us. Does the fullness of the Spirit mean wholeness for a holy heart? Yes and no. Because life is a journey of changing cir-

cumstances and new challenges that continue to test our faith, we grow from wholeness to wholeness in the fullness of the Spirit. At each stage of life, for instance, our holiness comes under a different test. The test of a holy heart during the height of career is quite different from the test that comes at the time of retirement. This fact is not cause for doubt or despair. Rather, it gives our Christian life the anticipation of high adventure. Just as the newborn believer is as whole in the Spirit as a babe in Christ can be, so the longtime believer who is advanced in the faith can have a holy heart with room to grow. Each can anticipate becoming more Christlike throughout a lifetime, and each can anticipate completion in Christ at the time of death. Perfection awaits our glorification.

21st-Century Leadership Initiatives

Practical steps are now needed to make the experience of the holy heart a present possibility for all believers. Wesleyan leaders need to consider their steps:

1. Simplify the doctrine. Rather than getting caught up in timing, wording, and procedure, we need to go to biblical basics that make holiness an affirmative and pervasive growth experience that all believers can anticipate.

2. Teach the total. Rather than stressing one step or another in the development of a holy heart, whether it is event or experience, we need to communicate the totality of the journey toward spiritual maturity.

3. Preach the promise. Although growth toward holiness is a process, the event of being filled with the Spirit is a gift of God that is promised by Christ and proven by the work of the Holy Spirit. All apologies, then, should be put aside, and the truth should be preached but always within the context of a natural step along the path of a deepening hunger for the fullness of the Holy Spirit. Avoid, at all costs, a lockstep system in which individual differences in spiritual development are not recognized.

4. Disciple for development. Our programs for spiritual nurture must coincide with the wholeness model of holiness. Just as John Wesley organized his classes, bands, and societies with the spiritual growth of believers in mind, we must have teaching and learning experiences for each step on the path to wholeness. Furthermore, as a Christian education curriculum, provision must be made for advancement, remedial work, and dropouts among believers. As with Wesley, the goal is a measure of spiritual maturity with increasing responsibility for leadership in the Church and its witness of social compassion.

5. **Expect the evidence.** If our expectations for the evidence of a holy heart are low, they will be fulfilled. But if our expectations are high, they will also be fulfilled. A generation ago, our expectations were too high because they were rigid and unrealistic. Now, they are too low. Believers can wallow around in spiritual immaturity for years without a call to accountability. Why not expect growth in the fruits of the Spirit? Why not expect a life of praise, passion for God, zeal for righteousness, and self-giving for others? Why not expect evidence of the "fullness of the Spirit-filled, Spirit-empowered life"?

6. **Model the message.** As always, our preaching and teaching about the experience of a holy heart rises or falls on evidence in the lives of our leaders. As Henri J. M. Nouwen wrote in his book *In the Name of Jesus,* a Christian leader must live out the meaning of unconditional love, vulnerable love, and trusting love in the name and for the sake of Jesus Christ.[10] True holiness can never be faked. Our people have a nose for the genuine when it comes to the sensing in depth the authenticity of a holy heart. They do not expect their leader to be perfect, but they do expect the compassion of unconditional love, the risk of vulnerable love, and the assurance of trusting love. As the heart of holiness is holiness of the heart, our leaders must show the way.

Metaphors are often used to help us clarify a complicated idea, especially when a paradox is involved. Paul Rader, president of Asbury College and retired International Commander of the Salvation Army, has traced some of the metaphors that have been used to explain the meaning of holiness and a holy heart. The metaphors include extraction of the root of sin, purification of the subconscious mind, crucifixion of self, resurrection of life, magnetic drawing of the Spirit, intimacy of relationship with the transcendent God, glow of healthfulness, and freedom from soul disease. Rader adds his own metaphor with the idea of reprogramming the software of the soul. According to this image, the computer is set up, the program is ready, and the CD is in place. All we need to do is make the decision and click on "Enter." According to our model of wholeness for the holy heart, I would recommend that we first instruct the program to "Select All" and then press "Enter."

8 The Celebration of a Holy Day

 Whatever happened to the holy day? Of all of the disciplines of the Church in the generation past, none has succumbed so easily to the insidious invasion of the Radical Self. Our observance of the Sabbath has been reduced to a tip of the hat to the holy God. The response to the question, "Whatever happened to our holy day?" is that the pendulum of Sabbath observance has swung wildly from the legalism of the past to the license of the present. Certainly, those of us who remember prohibitions against working, buying, and playing on the Sabbath day will resonate with this answer. One of the major adjustments that my wife and I had to make during the early years of our marriage was to resolve conflicting restrictions on Sabbath activity. Janet, a daughter of the manse, could play games but not study on Sunday. I, son of an equally conscientious lay household, could study on Sunday, but I couldn't play games. We resolved the issue by deciding that our children could do both.

Such reactions against past prohibitions may seem to be the most obvious answer for the liberty that Christians now enjoy on the Sabbath day. But more is at stake than freedom from legalism. We must come to grips with biblical truth regarding the Sabbath. Immediately, we are confronted with the ring of truth regarding the nature of the holy God, the theology of creation, the fourth commandment of the Mosaic Law, the fulfillment of that Law in the ministry of Jesus Christ, the timing for His resurrection, the witness of the New Testament Church, and the meaning of the Sabbath for the final consummation in the Book of Revelation. In other words, the holy day is threaded through the Word of God from beginning to end. We dare not let it become the symptom of our submission to the Radical Self. So rather than blaming the legalism of the past for the license of the present, we should be diagnosing the disease as another bit of evidence that the Radical Self has invaded the center of our faith and that the infection is pervading the body politic.

It is time to restore the full and affirmative meaning of the Sabbath day for the church of the 21st century.

Retracing Biblical Truth

While our experience may bring up a host of negative connotations about the observance of the Sabbath day, biblical truth tells us just the opposite. As we have already stated, the affirmative meaning of the holy day is threaded throughout Scripture from beginning to end and reaffirmed in history from beginning of creation to the end of time.

The Sabbath is inherent in creation. God himself established the Sabbath principle when He rested from the work of creation on the seventh day. Although He did not need the rest, He stopped to reflect on His work as part of the rhythm of life to which all human beings are attuned. In my book *Love Your Work* this rhythm is seen as the cycle of work, rest, worship, and play. Although God had no one to worship, His reflection at the end of each creative day and His pronouncement that His work was "very good" carry with them the "observation" and the "remembrance" that defines our worship. Also, we may not think of God at play, but when He blessed His creation and declared it holy, it takes no stretch of the imagination to sense the spontaneity of play in His blessing and the joy of play in celebrating His work as "holy."

There is nothing negative about the Sabbath day in the creation story. Instead, we see the Sabbath as the focal point in the rhythm of life that reflects the very image of God in us. To rest on the seventh day is essential to the wholeness of life. The rhythm is built into our being as a gift of God. To disrupt that rhythm is to destroy our health and demolish our wholeness. Therefore, when the Radical Self takes over our holy day and substitutes the worship of self-interest, the rhythm is broken and the breakdown begins. If this sounds like a typical Evangelical apologetic for a biblical truth that is limited to those who believe, consider the research finding Marva Dawn cites in her book *Keeping the Sabbath Wholly.* Juan-Cardos Lerman, professor at the University of Arizona, found that the "human clock" has the biological need for rest every seventh day in order to refresh itself. While our daily clock is built on the 24-hour cycle, our biological clock is built on a 25-hour cycle. So Lerman contends that we need a day off every seven days for our biological clock to catch up with our time clock so body, mind, and spirit can catch up with itself.[1] Although biblical truth needs no scientific confirmation, Lerman's observation coincides with the Word of God and our own intuitions. Each of us knows harmony when we are in the rhythm of life as well as the breakdown when the beat is broken.

The Sabbath is commanded in the Mosaic Law. The sequence and interrelationship of the first four commandments of the Mosaic Law are not accidental. After God commands "You shall have no other gods before me" (Exod. 20:3), He continues with two negative injunctions, "You shall not make for yourself an idol" and "You shall not misuse the name of the LORD your God" (vv. 4, 7). Then He turns to the great affirmation, "Remember the Sabbath day by keeping it holy" (v. 8).

A direct connection exists between worship of the holy God and the remembrance of His holy day. Thus when the Radical Self refuses to let God be God, it also robs Him of the honor that is due Him. The Sabbath is the object of contest. After re-creating the holy God in its own image, the Radical Self turns the holy day into an idol of its own making. Because the Sabbath symbolizes the gift of time God has given to us, the insatiable appetite of the Radical Self must gobble up the hours as a show of domination.

What a price we have paid! Not only have we shrunk the holy God down to an image of our own size, but we have also desecrated His holy day by worshiping the idols of the Radical Self that we have erected in the spiritual marketplace. Working rather than resting, doing rather than becoming, getting rather than giving, forgetting rather remembering, alienating rather than relating, producing rather than playing, succeeding rather than loving, and grousing rather than celebrating are all idols cast in the role of demons who have rushed into the vacuum created by the desecration of God's holy day.

The Sabbath is fulfilled in the grace of Jesus Christ. Once the image of the holy God has been shrunken to our size and the honor of His holy day given to idols of the marketplace, it is just a short step to then justify the motives of the Radical Self. How often have you heard Jesus' words "The Sabbath was made for man, not man for the Sabbath" (Mark 2:27) used to excuse doing whatever we want to do on Sunday? As usual, it is a distortion of the truth and an example of a scriptural text taken out of context. Jesus had to use radical words to counter the radical requirements the Pharisees had imposed on Sabbath observance. God will not allow the Sabbath to become an idol in His place anymore than He will allow the Radical Self to be elevated to the level of a competing god. But make no mistake about the whole truth. Jesus came to fulfill the Mosaic Law, not destroy it. Within the commandment "Remember the Sabbath day by keeping it holy" is the promise of grace. When Jesus stood up in the synagogue on the Sabbath day to give His inaugural address from the text of Isa. 61, He affirmed the full biblical meaning of the Sabbath (see Luke 4:16-30). By being in the synagogue on the seventh day, He was following God's example of resting on the Sabbath. By taking His text from Isaiah, He was confirming the Sabbath principle of the Law that made every seventh year a time for letting the soil lie fallow and canceling all debts. By introducing His ministry as the year of jubilee (the year after "seven times seven years" [see Lev. 25:8-13]) in which the poor are forgiven their debts, the blind see, the bound are released, and the bruised are given the courage to go on, He was announcing the salvation of the world as the ultimate purpose of Sabbath truth.

The Sabbath is enriched in the Epistles. Because the Jews had set up Sabbath regulations as a barrier to faith in Christ, the apostles did not overemphasize the observance of the day in their writings. It is significant, however, that Paul urged the Christians at Galatia and Corinth to set aside funds, on the first day of the week, as a collection to help the impoverished members of the Church in Jerusalem (1 Cor. 16:1-4). Also we remember so vividly the setting for John's writing of the Book of Revelation when he said, "On the Lord's Day I was in the Spirit" (Rev. 1:10). While there is little doubt about their diligence in observing the first day of the week in celebration of the Resurrection, their greater contribution is the evidence of Sabbath principles infusing their writings. Using the description of the New Testament Church in Acts 2:42-47 as an example, we see the spiritual meaning of the Sabbath fully displayed. Marva Dawn gives us a fourfold pattern for observing the Sabbath that can be readily seen in this description. *Ceasing* their work, they worshiped by devoting themselves "to the apostles' teaching and to the fellowship, to the breaking of bread and to prayer" (v. 42). *Resting* before the Lord, we are not surprised to read that they were refreshed in body, mind, and soul when "Everyone was filled with awe, and many wonders and miraculous signs were done by the apostles" (v. 43). *Embracing* each other as one in Christ, "All the believers were together and had everything in common," with the natural extension into loving others as they loved themselves—"Selling their possessions and goods, they gave to anyone as he had need" (vv. 44-45). *Feasting* followed with the expressions of joy found in the words "ate together with *glad* and sincere hearts, *praising* God and *enjoying* the favor of all the people" (vv. 46-47, emphasis my own).[2] The Church of Pentecost shows us what Christ meant by the fulfillment of the Law in the Sabbath day.

Throughout the Epistles and letters of the New Testament, then, Sabbath principles infuse the text like a radioactive isotope inserted into the bloodstream. Every cell, even at the outer extremities of the body, is affected. So it is in the New Testament churches. The spirit of the Sabbath influences the whole Body as it works, worships, rests, and celebrates.

In Hebrews, the meaning of Sabbath "rest" comes to full fruition as the metaphor for holiness. Even though past generations had failed to enter into the Sabbath rest promised by God because of a lack of faith, His promise is still good as He speaks: "There remains, then, a Sabbath-rest for the people of God; for anyone who enters God's rest also rests from his own work, just as God did from his" (4:9-10). Although "rest" may be open to various interpretations, the spiritual meaning is evident. God intends His people to claim the promise of shalom for the Sabbath day. We may think of "shalom" as a word that is used as a substitute for "peace" when two friends say good-bye. While its root meaning is "peace," it is more than that. Shalom, as Marva Dawn defines it, "begins in reconciliation with God and continues in reconciliation with our sisters and brothers—even our enemies. Moreover, shalom designates being at peace with ourselves, health, wealth, fulfillment, satisfaction, contentment, tranquility, and—to sum it all up—wholeness."[3] (To make shalom even more beautiful, Dawn suggests that we think of God spreading the tent of His peace over us and filling our dwelling with His holy presence.[4] When the children of Israel were wandering in the wilderness, God's presence covered them like a tent and His glory filled the place (Exod. 40:34-38). Using that same image, John wrote that Jesus' "tabernacled [or pitched his tent] among us" (John 1:14, literal translation). And not to be forgotten is John's revelation of the final Sabbath when He who "sits on the throne will spread his tent over [his people]" (Rev. 7:15). Of all of the definitions of holiness, none is more vivid or more inviting than the image of dwelling in the presence of God with His peace covering us like a tent and His fullness embracing every relationship of life. This is what makes the Sabbath God's holy day.

In its biblical context, the celebration of the Sabbath is one of the greatest affirmations of our faith. Negative images of past legalism give way to the richest expressions of God's grace at work in the lives of His people. By worshiping together on the Sabbath, we let God be God. By resting from our work, we restore the rhythm of creation by which we are made whole. By observing the holy day, we give the Church its distinctive witness in a secular society. By entering into the tent of His peace on the Sabbath day, we take shalom into every attitude and action of the week. By coming together on God's day, we become a community of faith with reconciliation in all relationships. By making the Sabbath a day of celebration, we show our gratitude for His blessings with praise and thanksgiving.

These rich spiritual benefits await us in the 21st century. We call upon our leaders to show us the way.

21st-Century Leadership Initiatives

None of us wants to return to the idolatry of the Sabbath created by the Pharisees of Jesus' time or to let the influence of the Radical Self continue to rob us of its relationship to holiness and wholeness. Our alternative is to seek the biblical balance between the rigidity of law and the freedom of license. The following leadership initiatives will give us a start.

1. **We must become students and teachers of Sabbath principles as revealed in the whole Word of God.** Bits and pieces of understanding for God's holy day will invariably lead to half-truths with the danger of idolatry or ignorance. To see the meaning of the Sabbath as integral to the whole Word of God from Genesis to Revelation is to revolutionize our viewpoint. To understand how the Sabbath relates to the work of creation, the spirit of the Law, the expression of grace, and the evidence of holiness is to make us long for the fullness of its meaning. This is a lost message among us that our leaders must recover.

2. **We must become intentional about Sabbath observance.** So much slippage has taken place in our attendance to the holiness of the Lord's day that we must take intentional steps to redeem its time. The positive response to the development of spiritual disciplines is in our favor. Richard Foster, in *Celebration of Discipline,* includes Sabbath observance as one of the "disciplines of engagement"

that we need to cultivate in our journey to spiritual maturity. Even then, it will not be easy to become intentional about keeping the Sabbath holy. A secular society dominated by the Radical Self has manifold weapons trained against the Sabbath day. The pressures of working, buying, selling, playing, advertising, and entertaining all militate against us. To hold one day holy may seem impossible in the contemporary society. Seventh-Day Adventists and Mormons show us otherwise. Someway, somehow, we must have the mind of the Spirit in knowing how to put Sabbath principles to work in the modern world without falling back into the legalism of the past. As a spiritual discipline for churches and our people, we need to ask, "How do the Sabbath principles of ceasing, resting, embracing, and feasting relate to our spiritual growth in the Church and our Christian witness in the world?" Although the answers will vary from place to place, the enactment of Sabbath principles will be transforming.

3. **We must relate the holy day to a holy people.** Because holiness is wholeness, the holy day is inseparable from a holy people. Whether referring to the rhythm of creation, the cycle of the Sabbath, or the pulse beat of shalom, the message of wholeness keeps coming through. God's promise that there is a rest reserved for His people, a rest into which we can enter by faith, must come back as our hope. To dwell in the "tent of peace" under the cover of God's presence in every aspect of life is another description of biblical holiness that begins with our worship on His holy day.

4. **We must make celebration the theme of our Sabbath day.** Early Christians set aside the first day of the week for remembering the Resurrection and celebrating the newness of life in Christ. Our worship services should ring with sights and sounds of that same celebration. The joy should continue in expressions of forgiveness, evidence of reconciliation, and offerings of self-sacrifice. Extending the theme even further, the celebration should include feasting together as the family of God in both the church and the home. The Mormons do many things right, including the common provision for the needy among them, the weekly provision for the family gathering, and the gracious provision for inviting outsiders to be a part of the intimate family. They have something to teach us.

Celebrating the Sabbath is never an end in itself. As the message of the Resurrection is the self-sacrifice of Christ for us, our celebration leads to self-sacrifice for others. Self-giving works of compassion in the name of Jesus Christ put the Radical Self in its place as leading to the dead end of joyless existence. When Christians celebrate the Sabbath, all hell shudders.

Again, much more could be said about leadership initiatives for celebrating God's holy day. Whatever we do to restore the biblical meaning of the day, our desire should be to be known as Sabbath people. So much awaits us by returning to Sabbath observance and practicing Sabbath principles. If we do, the greatest benefit is yet ahead. When Isaiah spoke of his vision for the New Zion in the final chapters of his prophecy, he included this promise:

"If you keep your feet from breaking the Sabbath and from doing as you please on my holy day, if you call the Sabbath a delight and the LORD's holy day honorable, and if you honor it by not going your own way and not doing as you please or speaking idle words, then you will find your joy in the LORD, and I will cause you to ride on the heights of the land and to feast on the inheritance of your father Jacob." The mouth of the LORD has spoken *(Isa. 58:13-14).*

Is the mouth of the Lord speaking again?

9 The Embrace of a Holy Family

The Radical Self is most destructive of human relationships. Its devastation is well known and well documented in the society at large. True to form, the entertainment media has caught the high tide of selfishness and ridden it into *Survivor*-type shows that make winners of the exalted self. Of course, the media claims it is reflecting the self-interest that is prevalent in the general society. With marketing and money in mind, we hear them plead once again, "We are only giving the public what it wants." They are not alone. The same lame excuse is used to justify the marketing thrust of churches, schools, and businesses that promote radical self-interest under the guise of serving the needs of prospective parishioners, students, and customers. The future will bode no better. With the advent of more sophisticated information technology, the "customer" will be able to package religion, education, or products according to the wishes and demands of self-interest. In this brave new world of the Radical Self, interpersonal relationships requiring commitment and responsibility are shunted into a secondary position, if they are considered at all.

Even more devastating is the pervasive influence of the Radical Self. Beginning at the cornerstone of a civil society, the Radical Self chips away at the common good in our laws and legislation. Provincialism in world affairs, parochialism at home, and privatism among persons are all side effects of this attitude. This intensive self-interest challenges "community life" and sacrifice for the common good. Worst of all, when "self as king" invades our primary institutions of home, church, and school, they become arenas where gladiatorial contests of competing self-interests rage to the death. Fathers turn against children, husbands against wives, brothers against brothers, and sisters against sisters.

How can the Body of Christ respond to the exaltation of the Radical Self as its influence courses through every cell of our society? The answer is a radical corrective for the sin of self-interest and a pervasive affirmation of sacrificial love as the antidote for its wholesale corruption of institutions and individuals. Our hope is in the family of God and the Body of Christ.

UNITY IN THE BODY

In the Epistle to the Ephesians, the apostle Paul writes, "Make every effort to keep the unity of the Spirit through the bond of peace" (4:3). He becomes more specific. He identifies the meaning of unity—"one body" because there is "one Spirit" (v. 4), "one hope . . . one faith, one baptism" because there is only one Lord (v. 5), and one family because there is only "one God and Father of [us] all" (v. 6). Despite a history of division and disunity in the Church at all levels, the fact remains that God intends His Body to be one.

The "oneness" of the Church is reinforced by the metaphor of the human body Paul describes in 1 Cor. 12:12-27: "The body is a unit, though it is made up of many parts; and though all its parts are many, they form one body. So it is with Christ. For we were all baptized by one Spirit into one body."

On this fundamental truth, the apostle builds his case for dealing with differences in the functions, gifts, and callings of the members of the Body of Christ. The functions of the foot, the ear, and the eye are all differentiated parts but still part of one body (vv. 14-27). The gifts of wisdom, knowledge, faith, healing, miracles, prophecy, tongues and the interpretation of tongues are also noted for their individuality, but still working as one and given by the same Spirit (vv. 4-11). The same image is used for different callings in the work of the Church—apostles, prophets, teachers, workers of miracles, healers, servants, administrators, and speakers in tongues (vv. 28-31). Ahead of the listing, Paul again gives the reminder, "Now you are the body of Christ, and each one of you is a part of it" (v. 27). Anticipating the functions, gifts, and callings that can divide us, Paul presses home the point that the Body of Christ is an organism that works on the principle of unity in diversity. Furthermore, under the guidance of the Spirit, it is healthy and on the move when all parts are functioning as one. Like the human organism, if one part is sick or rebellious, there is the natural thrust to bring the body back into wholeness and health.

The principle of unity in diversity is extended in the image of one family under the Fatherhood of God. But now, the metaphor changes from the body to the bridegroom. Both of these responses are found in the fifth chapter of Ephesians, a controversial chapter dealing with family relationships. After commanding husbands to love their wives, the apostle writes, "just as Christ also loved the church and gave Himself up for her; that He might sanctify her, having cleansed her by the washing of water with the word, that He might present to Himself the church in all her glory, having no spot or wrinkle or any such thing; but that she should be holy and blameless" (vv. 25-27, NASB). All human relationships, corporate in the Church and individual in persons, are to be guided by the example of Christ. It begins with self-sacrifice for the individual, and it results in sanctification for the Body of Christ. In this truth, we see the oneness and the wholeness that characterize the holy family of God.

Time and time again, the Scriptures make clear that holiness begins with death to self. Christ, however, takes us one step farther. Following His example, sanctification, cleansing, glory, purity, and holiness come to the Church when leaders give themselves sacrificially to those they love. From their example, this holy family demonstrates unity in a widening range of the diversity of relationships.

UNITY IN THE FAMILY

The bond between husbands and wives is the human relationship that mirrors the image of Christ as the Bridegroom and the Church as His bride. Creation is the initial guide for this relationship. As controversial as it may be in an age that presses for equality or the reversal of roles, the scripture is clear that wives are to submit themselves to their husbands because the male was created first and that the husband is to love his wife as he loves himself because Christ loves the Church and gave himself for it (see Eph. 5:22-33). While creation is the initial guide for defining these roles, the greater principle is the consecration of love by which Christ, the Bridegroom, gives himself for His bride, the Church. Sacrificial love, not domination or submission, is the motive for oneness in the marriage relationship.

The relationship between parents and children is closely aligned with that of husband and wife in the conjugal family. For children, "Honor your father and mother" is a commandment of great significance (see 6:1-3). Fathers, in turn, are admonished to train and instruct their children in the way of the Lord instead of frustrating them with moral and spiritual ambiguity (see v. 4). Although the parent-child relationship involves superiority and subordination more than the husband-wife relationship, the principle of sacrifice and love still prevails.

So, in the first and most important of human relationships, members of the conjugal family show God's love when they exemplify a diversity of roles and obey the Spirit. For husbands and wives, the unifying words are "love" and "submission"; for fathers and children, they are "obey" and "instruct."

Unity of Generations

In addition to the oneness of the conjugal family, the Scriptures also address the generational family. Joel's prophecy "In the last days, God says, I will pour out my Spirit on all people. Your sons and daughters will prophesy, your young men will see visions, your old men will dream dreams" (Acts 2:17; see Joel 2:28) is often quoted as the promise for Pentecost. Lost in the promise may be the picture of the multigenerational family of God. No generation is neglected. Young, middle-aged, and elderly will experience the outpouring of the Spirit, and each will play a unique role in a Great Awakening. The young are the visionaries, the middle-aged are the prophets, and the elderly are the dreamers. Another way to see the promise is to align the generations with the three sections in the outline of this book. The elderly are the dreamers who have the "sight of reality" from the past; the middle-aged are the prophets who have the "insight of truth" for the present; and the young are the visionaries who have the "foresight of hope" for the future.

Unity of Ethnicity, Status, and Gender

The apostle Paul is a realist. Knowing where the unity of the Body of Christ can be broken, he acknowledges the diversity of ethnicity, status, and gender. With bold pen, he declares, "You are all sons of God through faith in Christ Jesus, for all of you who were baptized into Christ have clothed yourselves with Christ" (Gal 3:26-27). Under this caveat, he makes the unequivocal statement, "There is neither Jew nor Greek, slave nor free, male nor female, for you are all one in Christ Jesus" (v. 28). He gets himself into trouble on each count. Jews are enraged by his insistence that the Greeks or Gentiles are now full heirs to salvation in Jesus Christ without having to jump through the hoops of Jewish ritual. Perhaps not in his day, but certainly within the last 200 years, Paul's pronouncement that men and women are neither "slave nor free" in the family of God cut cross grained against vested interests of slave owners who were also professed Christians. With the same pronouncement, he exposed the evil of entrenched attitudes of ethnic prejudice across the world among members of the Christian community.

The same can be said for the division between male and female. Although Paul uses the masculine designation for certain roles based on function, gift, or calling, he wastes no words here to say that any discrimination of persons based on gender is a violation of the "oneness" of the family of God. His concluding statement leaves no doubt about his position on the unity of all members in the Body of Christ, regardless of ethnicity, status, or gender. He writes, "If you belong to Christ, then you are Abraham's seed, and heirs according to the promise" (v. 29). In other words, in Christ we are all full members of God's family and heirs with a full share of His promise. By spiritual heredity and legal inheritance, we are one.

Unity of Hospitality

The family of God finds its strength in its oneness. To be a member is to have a sense of belonging, an assurance of being loved, and a promise of being praised. From this base of strength, however, the children of God are called to care for their own, particularly those who are identified as widows and orphans along with those who are poor and needy. James writes, "Religion that God our Father accepts as pure and faultless is this: to look after orphans and widows in their distress and to keep oneself from being polluted by the world" (James 1:27). This working principle has deep roots in the Old Testament law where God said, "Do not take advantage of a widow or an orphan" (Exod. 22:22). Jesus reinforced this principle when He pronounced judgment on the scribes who *devour widows' houses* by exorbitant fees and unfair pledges (Luke 20:47, emphasis added). The post-Pentecostal church then affirmed the principle in the demonstration of selling their possessions and holding all things common so they could give to everyone who had need. Those who dispute the process fail to understand the motivation behind the action. With the coming of the Holy Spirit, the great commandment is fulfilled not only as self dies and the love of God fills the soul but also as self is sacrificed in love for others. Whenever we speak of unity in diversity for the family of God, we can trace the oneness and the wholeness to the death to self and the sacrifice of love.

While the family of God meets the needs of its members first, it cannot become self-contained and self-sustaining. Out of Old Testament law comes the duty to strangers. In Lev. 19:34, the Israelites are reminded, "The alien living with you must be treated as one of your native-born. Love him as yourself, for you were aliens in Egypt. I am the LORD your God." In direct contradiction to the Radical Self, we who are members of the family of God must remember that we were once aliens, strangers, outcasts, and nameless people. Hospitality is not an onerous obligation imposed by God. It is an act of gratitude for the love of God and a lost art that must be recovered in the family of God.

UNITY OF CONDITION

A greater stretch of diversity for the family of God—even beyond strangers—includes those people who threaten us. These are the ones whose condition in life turns us against them. Matt. 25:35-46 specifically lists these people for whom we will be held responsible in the final Judgment. On the list are the hungry and thirsty whom we *dislike* because we must share with them, the homeless whom we *despise* because they will not work, the naked whom we *detest* because of their exposure, and the sick and imprisoned whom we *dread* because of their danger to us. Yet the Lord answers the puzzled inquiry of those who minister to these people and those who do not, "I tell you the truth, whatever you did for one of the least of these . . . you did for me" (v. 40). For our sakes, He was hungry, thirsty, homeless, naked, sick, and imprisoned. Thus for His sake we do the same for those who are the least among us.

The ultimate test of our strength as the family of God comes with Jesus' command, "Love your enemies and pray for those who persecute you, that you may be sons of your Father in heaven" (5:44-45). Whereas the hungry, thirsty, homeless, naked, sick, and imprisoned are passive threats to us, our enemies are the activists in antagonism. How will we respond to those who hate us? Diversity is no longer a matter of differences; it is a matter of survival. Jesus gives us fair warning about these enemies. He tells His disciples, "All men will hate you because of me" (Luke 21:17). Here is where the extended love of the Body of Christ is put to its greatest test. We must be known as those who love our enemies and pray for our persecutors. Why? Because this is how Jesus responds to His enemies and this is how we show that we are the sons and daughters of the Father in heaven. Like Jesus, our relationship with others begins in the home and ends on a cross.

21ST-CENTURY LEADERSHIP INITIATIVES

Diversity is quickly becoming one of the most pressing issues with which the Church must deal. Not long ago, the Church enjoyed the status of a leading institution in the society, shaping our moral character, developing our leadership, and serving in the relative comfort of homogeneous groupings within denominations. All that is now history. Diversity bordering on antagonism within families, generations, genders, ethnic groups, races, and socioeconomic classes now challenges the Church. Can the Church still exemplify the unity within diversity so vividly represented in Scripture by the images of the Body, the building, and the Bride? Such a question drives us to our knees because we are simply not ready for the challenge. Moreover, the question drives us back to the truth that our oneness in Christ is the result of crucifixion to self and resurrection in the power of the Holy Spirit. A holy family begins with holy people. From there, we must lead with these initiatives.

1. **Cultivate the "oneness" of a holy family.** Although the Church is better known for its fragmentation than its unity, we must never stop moving toward the biblical model. The current search for spirituality is more than a quest for self-actualization. It is also a search for the intimacy of a family where the individual can sense belonging, feel love, and win praise. Of all institutions, only the home along with the church has the potential to meet this universal human need. Time and time again, the biblical images of the Body, the building, and the Bride need to be brought forward in preaching and teaching as examples of the oneness of the Church. Around these images, the intimacy of the family should be encouraged by expressing belonging, feeling love, and winning praise. Practical demonstrations must follow as the church comes together around the hurts of family members, the disagreements among members, and the crises that threaten unity. But more than that, the family that stays together not only prays together but also celebrates together. Beginning with worship and continuing through family-type events, often centered in a common meal, the church is known by sounds of joy.

Undergirding all of these functions of a family must be a support system that is particularly suited to the needs of members who are outside the typical conjugal family. The biblical listing of widows and orphans is now extended to include single parents, single-parent children, single unmarrieds, blended families, senior citizens, and a wide range of disabled or abused people. By using the model of the conjugal family and applying its qualities to the Church as a whole, the vision of the family of God comes into view.

2. Put our "oneness" at risk. Only a family with a measure of maturity can reach beyond its comfort zone into an area of risk. In fact, the test of the strength of its unity is its ability to welcome into the family those who are threats and those who are enemies. This will not come easily. Only by intentional leadership action can the family risk its unity in what is called GAG ministries, meaning ministries "going against the grain." What is true for an individual is also true for a church. We learn the most, grow the greatest, and serve the best when going against the grain. Of course, we prefer "homogeneity" in the family and "readiness" of people for our evangelism. But what about the people at the final Judgment who fit neither category? They are more than hungry, thirsty, homeless, naked, sick, and imprisoned. They are the types who threaten us and whom we don't like. Yet if the family of God is to fulfill His redemptive purpose, there is no alternative. The ultimate test of every church and every congregation is to ask, "Where are we risking all in order to serve?" Few congregations will be able to answer this challenge, but those who do are demonstrating the meaning of God's family in which oneness and wholeness are two sides of the same coin called "holiness." The family that fails to reach beyond itself in wholeness will lose its oneness to bickering when it turns inward. Think of the alternative. The family of God that reaches beyond itself not only becomes stronger in its oneness but also finds enrichment for its wholeness. Just as a holy heart is known by self-giving love for others in adversity, a holy family is known by the evidence of "faith working through love" in diversity.

3. Open the family circle. At 8:57 A.M., eastern standard time, on September 11, 2001, my wife and I were on a cruise ship heading for the port of Kushadasi, Turkey. I had just finished sending an E-mail to the children telling them that we were safe after a news report that a suicide bomber had killed 2 policemen and wounded 22 shoppers in the Grand Bazaar of Istanbul—the exact spot we had visited a few days earlier. Returning to the cabin, Janet stared at CNN news, transfixed. She could only say, "A plane has crashed into the World Trade Center." Thinking back to the only event that matched that moment, I heard myself speak the words, "This is our 21st-century Pearl Harbor."

As we watched the disaster take place before our eyes, the captain's voice over the intercom announced the disaster and ordered the ship on highest security alert. Later, he invited all on board to observe three minutes of silence in memory of those killed by the terrorist act. For those minutes, my wife and I went to the gathering place at poolside on the promenade deck. With scores of other passengers, we sat in silence for three minutes, then held back the tears as we all sang "God Bless America." At the close, I looked up to see a Japanese family across the way. The father and daughter were sobbing and weeping without shame. In that moment, my racial and ethnic stereotypes crumbled. I surprised myself by saying, "No, this is not our 21st-century Pearl Harbor. These Japanese people love America as much as I do."

On our way home a few days later, we flew over the smoking site of the World Trade Center. As we observed the remains, we realized we had been protected from the full emotional impact because of our distance from home. With devilish accuracy, the terrorists had chosen the target that symbolized our security and our prosperity. Later, when the roster of the dead was released, I saw another symbol that had been attacked. Sixty-three nations were represented among those who died in the disaster. Complementing the crash of my racial and ethnic stereotypes on shipboard, I saw a microcosm of the human family unfold before my eyes. We are not only one at home but also one with the world.

Naturally, I began to transfer my new revelation into the context of the Church and our responsibility as Wesleyan leaders. Typically, the local church is a Body of Believers who fit into a narrow spectrum of race, education, social class, and economic status. Ministries of mercy abound, but in selected areas and through specialized agencies. The model must change. No longer do we have the luxury of a closed community with the expectation that the world will beat a path to our doorstep. No longer do we have the privilege of outsourcing our compassion through peripheral programs and external agencies. Transformation must take place at the core of our culture, namely, in the complexion and composition of our worshiping congregations. Except for a few static communities in rural settings, the character of our neighborhoods is changing before eyes. If our churches are to keep pace with this change, our congregations will mirror the diversity of racial, ethnic, educational, and economic differences. As usual, transformation is easier said than done. Evangelical Christians excel in ministries that fit the Bible Belt, the suburban setting, and the rural community. We are hardly known as champions of urban ministry. Yet as the terrorists proved in New York City, this is where the world turns. Among all of the challenges facing us as Wesleyan leaders, the transformation of the local congregation and the penetration of the city stand near the top. By deliberate design, the Body of Christ must be as diverse as our changing communities and as global as our shrinking world.

If we heed the wake-up call of September 11, 2001, we will see the Body of Christ taking on its New Testament identity and transforming the nature of the Church itself.

IN PRAISE OF DIVERSITY

Consider this note of praise. The Holy Spirit can be poured out upon a church as well as individuals. When He moves upon a church, oneness in diversity becomes its internal characteristic and wholeness in diversity becomes its external challenge. Diversity within the family of God begins with individual functions, gifts, and callings and extends to interpersonal relationships between husbands and wives, parents and children, men and women, the old and young, the rich and poor. Diversity in the society outside the immediate family of God is even more demanding. A widening gap of differences—racial, ethnic, gender-related, educational, and socioeconomic—tests both the oneness and the wholeness of the church that dares to reach out in the name of Jesus. This challenge includes the passive poor who threaten us, the alien stranger who needs us, and the active enemy who opposes us. The farther the church reaches out, the greater the need for the strength of oneness and the vision of wholeness that comes with the Spirit's fullness of love. The church divided internally lacks oneness, and the church withdrawing from external diversity lacks wholeness. So as believers are called to the experience of the holy heart, the church is called to the evidence of a holy family. In every relationship, we are called to love others, "just as Christ loved the church and gave himself up for her to make her holy, cleansing her by the washing with water through the word, and to present her to himself as a radiant church, without stain or wrinkle or any other blemish, but holy and blameless" (Eph. 5:25-27). A troubled world awaits this show of love.

10 The Witness of a Holy Sacrifice

 An old adage says, "You can tell Evangelicals how they ought to live, but you can't tell them how to vote or give their money."

Our dread of the subject of stewardship and our independence about dollars have an ally in the attitudes of the Radical Self. Each of us has two invaluable resources that can determine our destiny. One is the resource of *time* that must be redeemed. As we have already seen, if the Radical Self robs us of holy time on the Sabbath day, it will conquer the days of our week and the years of our lives. The other is the resource of *money* that must also be redeemed. Our shares are unequal, but our stewardship is the same. If the Radical Self dominates the center of our economic interests and pervades our economic decisions, it will conquer us.

THE ECONOMICS OF SELF-INTEREST

Is the Radical Self winning? As beneficiaries of the greatest spurt of economic growth in human history, North American Christians are a prosperous people. Our possessions, our pensions, and our portfolios point to our wealth. Even in an economic recession aggravated by terrorist attacks, there are few of the very poor among us. Robert Fogel, in *The Fourth Great Awakening,* claims that a measure of "economic equity" has been achieved in the last 100 years as a result of the Third Great Awakening. He cites statistics showing that the number of people in North America lacking the fundamental needs of food, clothing, and shelter is at a minimum. The "level of poverty" based on income has been raised regularly above inflation, and the number of impoverished children, identified as the "new poor" among us, is being reduced each year.[1] But wealth and poverty are relative, not absolute, conditions. If the comparison between the rich and poor in North America is drawn, the gap continues to widen, not just in dollars but also in attitudes and aspirations. Henry David Thoreau once wrote, "The man is rich who makes his wants few." One of the tactics of the Radical Self is to stimulate our wants so that we are perpetually dissatisfied with our economic position even though our needs are met. Just an hour watching the ads on television shows us how our society is geared to creating dissatisfaction with our current status and making our possessions obsolete overnight. There is little doubt that the Radical Self dominates the economic world and pervades every aspect of our daily living. In a very real sense, even the richest among us is poor if the lust for "wants" is not satisfied.

THE CONFLICT WITH BIBLICAL STEWARDSHIP

Although the economics of the Radical Self are in direct contradiction to the principles of biblical stewardship, Evangelical Christians are both culprits of its wiles and victims of its seductive powers. Most obvious is the unapologetic preaching of a "prosperity gospel." Close behind comes the attitude, "What we have, we own." In such cases, whether we are rich or poor, money and possessions become idols that take the place of the holy God. Still another step in the shift away from biblical stewardship is for denominations and individual churches to be driven by economic interests that are reflected in budgets designed to protect "identifiable self-interest," a thoroughly secular attitude. George Hunter, professor of evangelism at Asbury Theological Seminary and an astute observer of denominations, asked a delegate to an annual conference, "What did you observe about the annual conference? Did anything surprise you?" The delegate answered, "Well, the whole organization seems set to provide for the fair compensation, vocational satisfaction, and graceful retirement of the ordained clergy!"[2] While clergy compensation is a legitimate subject, even among our clergy self-interest reveals itself when money takes over mission.

Look even deeper into the economic message being sent by our Christian ministries. A generation or two ago, most ministries of evangelism and outreach depended upon "faith" for financial viability. Today, with the advent of fund-raising as a sophisticated technique within the church and its institutions, there is little conversation about faith. In its place are "endowments" that are intended to assure freedom from financial worry in perpetuity. Under the glow of success among Evangelical ministries, attention has been turned from the daily dollar to deferred gifts. I speak from experience. In every institution of higher education where I served as president, we were just one generation away from a hand-to-mouth existence. So one of my presidential priorities was to assure a balanced operating budget so that we could turn to the task of raising endowments and seeking planned gifts. Basically, I don't believe that this direction is contrary to biblical stewardship unless our dependence shifts from faith to dollars. Endowments, rightly used, can free us for attention to spiritual leadership within our organizations and more effective ministries of outreach beyond our organizations. So far, history is against us. Too many Christian ministries have been spoiled by endowments. When funding is secure, faith takes on a different meaning. Consider the national debate over government funding for "faith-based charities" in order to serve better the needs of America's poor. At one time, "faith-based charities" meant ministries that were supported by "faith" gifts. Today, the term means those charities that have a "faith" position theologically but count on government funds for economic support. While the proposal has merit, reality tells us that economically driven motives always have their dark side.

EVANGELICAL ECONOMICS

Without going farther along the path where the Radical Self is blazing the trail, enough has been said to know that the Fourth Great Awakening has created a pitched battle between affluence and holiness. John Wesley foresaw this battle when he predicted that converts of true Christianity will "beget riches" as frugal and diligent stewards of financial resources. He was not advocating a "prosperity gospel." With his prediction, he also gave the warning that the consequences of riches result in a Christianity that is inconsistent with itself and, therefore, can sap the very foundations of the faith.

Wesley's warning resounds into the 21st century. Michael Hamilton has written an article in *Christianity Today* titled "We're in the Money!"[3] He gathers the facts that Evangelicals, including Holiness and Pentecostal types, are a wealthy people. The budgets and assets of our churches, parachurch organizations, media ministries, missionary movements, educational institutions, and book publishers prove his point. Yet in respect to these ministries, Evangelicals give only 4-8 percent of their income. To be sure, this is considerably more than the contributions of the general public or the gifts of mainline church members to their religious organizations. Nevertheless, it confirms the fact that Evangelicals have wealth from which they can give less than a tithe and still have more than 90 percent left for themselves. We are like the atheist who went to church and was confronted by the gospel. He said, "I came with a religious question on my mind and left with a spiritual question on my hands." When it comes to our affluence, we begin with an economic question on our minds and end with a spiritual question on our hands.

The question is further compounded when we look forward to the future. Evangelical Christians enjoy more than enough money to sustain a high standard of living. We are able to make investments and build estates that will be witnesses to our stewardship after our death. Even now, informed sources tell us that we will see the largest transfer of wealth in human history during the next generation. Estimates run as high as 17 trillion dollars that will be passed down from depression babies to baby boomers alone. As a member of the senior generation, I must ask myself how I apply the principles of biblical stewardship to that transfer for my children. More important yet, I must ask myself if I have transferred the *principles* of biblical stewardship to my children ahead of the dollars. The intrusion of the Radical Self into our economic planning and decisions does not help. As I come to grips with the issues in my own life, I can only pray that it is not too late to bring biblical stewardship back to the top of the agenda as a priority for Christian accountability.

A REFRESHER ON BIBLICAL STEWARDSHIP

Scores of books have been written on Christian stewardship using biblical principles. The popularity of the subject is indicative of the dilemma that many believers face in daily budgeting as well as long-term planning. Our purpose is not to repeat the sound biblical principles developed in many of these books, but to address the specific question of biblical holiness as it relates to our individual and institutional economics.

The Tithe—Our Required Minimum. Our responsibility as 21st-century Christians begins with our tithe. Although the command to give a 10th of all of the "first fruits" of production was given to the children of Israel, the principle has never been canceled. As noted earlier, even though Evangelical Christians are far more generous givers than the general public or mainline church members, our giving is still short of a tithe. If the principle of "first fruits" is applied, it probably means that overall giving is even less than 4-8 percent because of mental gymnastics that let us make other deductions, such as taxes, before giving.

To add to the story, the use of the tithe in our church budgets often fails to conform to the expectations of biblical stewardship. Most of us remember God's instruction to the Israelites to harvest 90 percent of their crops and leave a 10th for the poor to reap. If this is the first and fundamental purpose of tithing, there are few individuals or institutions that designate a tithe for the needs of the poor. In Deut. 12:17-19, we read the instructions to use the tithe for feasting and caring for the Levites, who were priests of the Lord. If our tithes were directed to these three purposes—feeding the poor, feasting as a family, and funding the care of clergy—what a difference it would make in our budget planning. To restore the tithe as a fundamental expectation for Evangelical Christians in the 21st century and to construct our budgets with priorities for feeding the poor, feasting in the family, and caring for the clergy is a revolution in the making.

The Offering—Our Graduated Gift. Ronald Sider, in his book *Rich Christians in an Age of Hunger,* proposes a graduated tithe for wealthy Christians. As wealth increases, the percentage of the tithe rises. The idea has merit, but not for the tithe. In teaching the lesson of the widow's mite, Jesus infers the same principle for the offerings that are given above the tithe. We remember the story. As Jesus is watching the rich putting their gifts into the Temple treasury, He also sees a poor widow give "two very small copper coins." "'I tell you the truth,' he said, 'this poor widow has put in more than all the others. All of these people gave their gifts out of their wealth; but she out of her poverty put in all she had to live on'" (Luke 21:1-4). While the tithe is fixed at 10 percent, our gifts should be given in relationship to our wealth. While the tithe is a required minimum, our gifts are limited only by the extent of our gratitude.

Jesus reinforces this principle of giving several times. For the rich young ruler, for instance, the only way he could break the grip that wealth had on his soul was to give it away. I recall being asked to consult with one of America's richest men on how to steward his wealth with gifts to worthy ministries. He had recently become a Christian and was seeking spiritual guidance. After a morning of conversation about the options, I decided to test his newfound faith by saying, "Maybe God wants you to give it all away." My startled host looked at me, chuckled, and then said, "I am not that much of a Christian yet." He was more honest than most of us.

In another instance, Jesus is speaking about the differences of privilege among people when they come to the final Judgment. Although He does not specifically mention wealth, it can certainly be inferred from His words: "From everyone who has been given much, much will be demanded; and from the one who has been entrusted with much, much more will be asked" (Luke 12:48b).

Our offerings are much more than meeting the obligation of privilege if we are blessed with resources beyond our needs. To show our gratitude, we give our gifts. No percentage or amount is required, but love has its own measure of giving. Is not this the moral of the story when the woman who had lived a sinful life interrupted dinner at a Pharisee's house in order to pour expensive perfume on Jesus' feet, wash them with her tears, and wipe them with her hair? Countering the Pharisee's criticism that she was a sinner who wasted precious perfume that could have been sold and given to the poor, Jesus answered, "I tell you, her many sins have been forgiven—for she loved much. But he who has been forgiven little loves little" (Luke 7:47). If this principle is applied to the size of our voluntary gifts beyond the tithe, most of us are ingrates. As our tithe indicates in whom we really put our trust, our gifts reveal whom we really love.

The Collection—Our Sacrificial Act. Biblical principles of stewardship take another step beyond the tithe and the gift in the form of special collections for urgent needs. Writing to the church at Corinth, the apostle Paul instructs all members to participate in a collection taken on the first day of each week for their impoverished brethren in the church at Jerusalem (see 1 Cor. 16:1-4). This is a delicate matter because neither church has riches and tension still remains between the Gentiles at Corinth and the Jewish Christians at Jerusalem. Paul is calling for an act of sacrifice, not only with the hope of reconciliation but also with the benefit of self-giving for both churches. Christians at Corinth will learn the joy of self-sacrifice, and Christians at Jerusalem will understand the meaning of sacrificial love. For both, it will be the evidence of death to self, love for God, and sacrifice for others—none other than the proof of holiness.

21st-Century Leadership Initiatives

Among all of the challenges mounted by the Radical Self, none is more formidable than the influence of affluence. The natural resistance to the teaching and application of the biblical principles of stewardship make the task even tougher. Yet if we are true to the Word and especially the teaching of Jesus, we have no choice. Biblical stewardship must have its place on our 21st-century agenda.

1. We must return to the biblical meaning of stewardship.
During recent years, a buzzword has become common in churches
and organizations. The word is "ownership." Perhaps as a reaction
against authority with its power of privileged information, people
have felt as if they were chattel slaves of an arbitrary system. In
many cases where episcopal authority or pastoral personality gives
people no voice, reform is needed. But once the pendulum began to
swing, the Radical Self took over. "Ownership" now means defiance
of authority and refusal to participate unless everyone is given a
voice and a vote. Behind this attitude is the protection of self-interest. Biblical stewardship is just the opposite. The starting point is to
remember that the word "economics" is a biblical word rooted in the
Greek term *oikonomos* and meaning "manager of the household." In
the parable of talents (Matt. 25:14-30), for instance, when Jesus
refers to the servants or stewards who were both wise and foolish,
He actually calls them "slaves." These are people who are the pos-
session of the master. They own nothing and yet are entrusted with
responsibility for managing their lord's investments. When he returns, they are held accountable for the use of the master's funds.
This is the mirror in which we must see ourselves as stewards of the
Master. Owning nothing, we are entrusted to manage all with full
accountability when He returns.

2. We must graphically demonstrate biblical stewardship. By
and large, we must confess that our preaching and teaching of biblical stewardship has been ineffective. Taken as a whole, members of
Evangelical Christianity do not even give a tithe. Perhaps the time
has come to teach by show-and-tell. Beginning with denominational
budgets, our leaders should be held accountable for planning those
budgets according to the principles of biblical stewardship. Because
a denominational budget is intended to be a financial picture of the
strategy and priorities of the ministry, it should be presented and reported as a dynamic expression of the denominational mission in action. Using the biblical principles of the tithe, for example, how
much is invested in the quality of pastoral leadership? Is there a
budget for celebration in the church? How much of the "first fruits"
are given to meet the needs of the poor? Go on to ask about the gifts
of love in offerings and the special collections that call for sacrifice.
How are these principles translated into dollars?

The same approach needs to be taken to the development and
presentation of local church budgets. A graphic presentation of a

mission-driven budget illustrating biblical stewardship is a tool for teaching that we need to discover. Most of all, we need to demonstrate biblical stewardship in our family budgets so that even the children can understand. If Christian parents prepared family budgets, perhaps in pie-shaped charts, showing income and expenses following the principles of biblical stewardship, a child would never forget seeing the slice of 10 percent for tithe along with the explanation that God came first. Norman Edwards, prominent fund-raising consultant for Christian organizations, goes one step further. He says that the best indicator of our faith is found in the stubs of our checkbook.[4] "Where your treasure is, your heart is also" is a truth as practical as our annual budgets and the stubs of our checkbooks.

3. We must reconnect biblical stewardship and biblical holiness. When self-interest intrudes into Christian stewardship, our scope of responsibility narrows, our decisions become selective, and our accountability is lost. The fact that the total giving of Evangelical Christians is less than a tithe speaks for itself. With more than 90 percent of our income dedicated to our own needs and wants, the signal is clear. Whatever we give to God looks more like a bribe to curry His favor or divert His wrath. Still, we claim the Old Testament promise of His blessings and our inheritance. We do not know what we are missing. Because tithing is a command, it must be restored as a spiritual discipline among God's people. Churches that dare to make tithing a requirement do not suffer from loss of members. In fact, they gain members because tithing is obedience to God and the starting point for growth in Christ.

In every community where I served as a college, university, or seminary president, I became involved in the United Way. For me, it was a way of witness with the leadership of the community, including the opportunity to remind them that People Helping People is a slogan with spiritual roots. I also learned something about effective fund-raising. The United Way works on the following progressive plan for its donors: (1) make a gift, (2) make a larger gift, (3) make a regular gift, (4) make a major gift, and (5) make a deferred gift.

Biblical stewardship involves a similar progressive plan. John Wesley's writings on this subject teach that our financial stewardship and our spiritual maturity go hand in hand. He backed up his teaching with a plan for systematic giving. His principles of growth and giving apply to us today. As we grow in grace, our stewardship matures from *tithes* as spiritual discipline to *offerings* as spiritual gratitude and on to *collections* as spiritual sacrifice.

Our two-thirds world churches are models for this truth. Out of their poverty, they give to sustain their ministries, support the poor among them, stretch their outreach at home, and then send missionaries to other parts of the world. They are showing us the way by going from the discipline of the tithe to offerings of love and collections of sacrifice. For them, biblical stewardship is inseparable from biblical holiness. If we are to strike a deathblow to the Radical Self in our society, we must follow those who are leading the way.

11 The Risk of Holy Compassion

 Compassion for others is the crowning virtue of Christian love. Compassion is also the practical demonstration of social holiness. The second greatest commandment, "Love your neighbor as yourself" (see Matt. 22:34-40; Mark 12:28-34), directly repudiates the Radical Self and everything for which it stands. But the archenemy of our souls is a master of strategy. Knowing that a frontal attack is futile, he chooses to outflank us with the wiles of self-interest in the guise of self-protection. Personal relationships, for example, lose the mutuality of commitment and become negotiated agreements. Even married couples who wouldn't think of a prenuptial contract but still negotiate their relationship fall into the trap of creating an adversarial climate in which self-interest is the underlying motive.

Relationships with institutions are particularly susceptible to the protection of self-interest. Commitment to the vision of the institution or loyalty to its mission becomes secondary to a formal contract based on "giving-getting." Even Christian ministries get caught in the spillover of this attitude. As a president of three Christian institutions of higher education over a period of 33 years, I never had a contract or a letter of agreement that served as a contract. I served at the pleasure of the board with no guarantees except the goodwill of Christian brothers. Times have changed. During the past 10 years I have served as a consultant for nine presidential searches for Christian organizations, primarily in higher education. Most candidates today expect a contractual agreement that defines their role in detail and focuses on the benefits of compensation, including severance in the event of dismissal. One president insisted on so many details that his contract required 27 pages! While my experience tells me that the candidates for presidencies in Christian ministries today are no less committed to Christ and His calling than those of my generation, I cannot help but wonder whether the Radical Self has outflanked us again. Potential leaders for Christian ministries who ask "What can I get for what I can give?" are burying a landmark of Christian service under the sands of self-protection.

Earlier, we noted that the lofty purpose of charitable giving has the blemish of self-interest. Anyone who has made proposals to a charitable foundation or a philanthropic person knows what is meant by "identifiable self-interest." Appeals for compassion fall upon deaf ears unless there is some connection between the request and the predetermined interest of the foundation or the philanthropist. Grantsmanship becomes gamesmanship as fund-raisers try to find the hook on which to hang their proposals. So whether the relationship is personal, institutional, or philanthropic, the ugly head of the Radical Self rears once again seeking dominance of the center and contamination of the whole.

THE CASE FOR CHRISTIAN COMPASSION

We must return to our basic premise. Wherever the Radical Self seeks dominance, we must be more radical in our willingness to die to self; and wherever self-interest has permeated the whole, we must be wholly holy in all of our relationships. As we have already seen, Christian compassion is an attitude and an act especially susceptible to the wiles of self-interest under the guise of self-protection. Thus we must pay close attention to Christ's teaching about compassion before we dare think about our agenda for the 21st century.

Compassion is a two-sided coin. John characterizes Jesus as a person "full of grace and truth" (John 1:14). In the balance of fullness, we realize that compassion may be as tender as grace and as tough as truth. Mercy and justice are partners in the same paradox. We tend to swing between the two extremes, parceling out heavy doses of mercy at one time and justice at another. Jesus, however, keeps the balance by the "fullness" of grace and truth. They work together, they complement each other, and, when the consequences are weighed, they leave no doubt about the fact that they are the fullest expression of compassionate love.

In the same vein, we speak of personal and social holiness, tending to overemphasize one while shortchanging the other. If we are to be wholly holy, however, we must find balance in the fullness of love that Jesus shows us.

COMPASSION FOR OUR FAMILY

Like the center of expanding concentric circles, compassion begins at home. Jesus feels that center of love so deeply that in His dying gasp He looks down from the Cross, sees His mother standing near John the beloved, and says, "'Dear woman, here is your son,' and to the disciple, 'Here is your mother.' From that time on, this disciple took her into his home" (John 19:26-27). With these words, Jesus is expressing the inseparable bond of love between a mother and a son. He is also confirming everything He teaches about loving relationships in the family of God, from the youngest child to the oldest widow.

Even though Jesus is rejected by His own brothers and sisters, He extends the image of the human family into spiritual dimensions. When told that His mother and brothers had come to see Him, He answers, "Who are my mother and my brothers?" Looking around the circle of his followers, He says, "Here are my mother and my brothers! Whoever does God's will is my brother and sister and mother" (Mark 3:31-34). Those who think He is an ungrateful son need to remember His words on the Cross. Jesus is creating the bond of love for a family of faith that is to become the basis for the New Testament Church. He is also establishing the responsibility of the family for the welfare of every member. With the fullness of grace in self-giving and fairness of truth in distribution, the needs of every member are to be met. Acts 2:44-45 is the direct of outworking of both sides of the coin of compassion: "All the believers were together and had everything in common. Selling their possessions and goods, they gave to anyone as he had need." Grace and truth, mercy and justice are one in this historic moment. The welfare of every member is not a burden but a blessing. Compassion for family is *to assure with fairness the total welfare of every member.*

THE COMPASSION FOR NEIGHBORS

As the concentric circles of human relationships extend beyond the family of faith, our neighbors come into view. Here are persons who are neither blood relatives nor believers in the faith. Our relationships may be as casual as talking over the backyard fence, meeting at the supermarket, or coming together in crisis. Yet these persons are embraced in the second great commandment that tells us we should "love our neighbors as ourselves." (see Matt. 19:19). An expert in the law asks the next question for us: "Who is my neighbor?" (Luke 10:29). Jesus answers with the parable of the Good Samaritan (see vv. 30-35). The story does not need repeating, but the moral does. We know neither the name, nationality, nor title of the man in the ditch who had been assaulted by thieves. We do know the titles and the nationalities of the three persons who came along the road. A priest, a Levite, and a Samaritan all see the plight of the victim and make a decision. While the esteemed priest and the privileged Levite go out of their way to avoid the beaten man, the despised Samaritan interrupts his journey to give himself and his resources in an act of compassion. After telling the story, Jesus turns the lawyer's question back to him, asking, "Which of these three do you think was a neighbor to the man who fell into the hands of robbers?" Without hesitation, the lawyer answers, "The one who had mercy on him." Jesus then confirms this truth with a universal mandate: "Go and do likewise" (vv. 36-37).

This parable wipes out all excuses for the neglect of a neighbor. In simplest terms, *a neighbor is another human being in need and compassion is to become personally involved in relieving that need without discrimination.* We are reminded that one of the spiritual outcomes of a Great Awakening is the evidence of disinterested benevolence. No matter how miserable or spiteful our neighbor may be, Christian compassion has no favorites.

Compassion for Our Enemies

To this point, compassion is a relatively low-risk expression of human nature at its best. Quite naturally, we will share ourselves with members of our families in order to assure their welfare, and the best side of us will often come forward to give relief to a neighbor in need. If only Jesus had stopped there, most of us could lay some claim to being compassionate persons. But Jesus knows our tendencies to justify ourselves. So when He describes the new spirit of the kingdom of God in His Sermon on the Mount, He draws a line of distinction between human compassion and Christlike compassion. The test is straightforward. Jesus says, "You have heard that it was said, 'Love your neighbor and hate your enemy.' But I tell you: Love your enemies and pray for those who persecute you, that you may be sons of your Father in heaven. . . . If you love those who love you, what reward will you get? Are not even the tax collectors doing that? And if you greet only your brothers, what are you doing more than others? Do not even pagans do that? Be perfect, therefore, as your heavenly Father is perfect" (Matt. 5:43-48).

Here is another example of what Lloyd Ogilvie calls the "hard sayings" of Jesus. To show compassion to our enemies and pray for our persecutors is impossible without the love that goes beyond the best of human resources. Jesus does not specify acts of compassion, but He does make it clear that citizens of His kingdom will take the initiative in responding to the hatred and persecution of their enemies with a show of love and a word of prayer. Later, Jesus identifies those enemies by saying, "All men will hate you because of me" (Matt. 10:22).

Luke, in his record of the same sermon, expands on the same subject. He hears Jesus say, "Love your enemies, do good to those who hate you, bless those who curse you, pray for those who mistreat you" (Luke 6:27-28). Citing examples, Luke tells us that this means turning the other cheek when beaten, being robbed of your coat, giving the thief the rest of your clothes, and even lending your enemy money without expecting a return. In each of these cases, the Radical Self is cringing. It is one thing to share with the family or to give relief to a neighbor, but to have the love that seeks no revenge, desires no retaliation, and expects no return can only be expressive of the compassion of Christ. As hard as it may be, *compassion for our enemies means taking the initiative with selfless love and letting God be the arbiter of justice.*

Looking back on these three relationships, we see both grace and truth, mercy and justice, at work. As compassion advances from the love of family to neighbors and enemies, the need for self-sacrifice increases. With the family, we share all; with our neighbors, we share some; and with our enemies, we give it all away. The risk also increases. Family members will return our love, neighbors will say "Thank you," and enemies will only strike again. No wonder that Jesus says at the conclusion of His teaching on compassion, "Be perfect, therefore, as your heavenly Father is perfect" (Matt. 5:48). The perfection of compassion is to show selfless love at all levels of human relationships, from the family to the enemy. For good reason, we can speak of "holy" compassion.

WHEN THE CHURCH IS THE CHURCH

How often have we pleaded, "Let the church be the church?" Behind the plea is the wish that the church could be free from the grime of a dirty world in order to give its attention to ministries that are purely redemptive in character. If this is our outlook, we are deluded. A redemptive church is a church at risk.

Our morning newspaper carried two stories that leave no doubt about that risk. One story was a report from Afghanistan where two American volunteers with the Shelter Now ministry for children gave a Bible to a Muslim family and showed a film on Jesus. Because Islam recognizes the Bible as a holy book and Jesus as one of the prophets, they reasoned that they were breaking no law. Afghan authorities felt otherwise. The two young women were arrested by the Taliban, enforcers for Muslim purity. Despite international protests, they face a private trial followed by the possibility of a public execution or serving as hostages for protection against American air attack. The Muslim family has also been arrested and condemned for listening. When the church is *the* Church, there is a price to be paid.

The second story came from our neighborhood in the Northwest. Laymen of the Lighthouse Free Methodist Church in Lynnwood, Washington, took seriously Jesus' call for compassion and began visiting prisoners in the state penitentiary. One prisoner, James Elldredge, was particularly responsive to their ministry. After his release from prison in 1995, the church took him in, providing housing for him and employing him as a church custodian. For three years he faithfully attended church, worked with diligence, and developed a relationship that led to marriage. In 1998, however, he became obsessed with hate for a woman who had warned his future wife about his background. Going to the woman's home one evening, he promised her and a female friend gifts and dinner if they would accompany him to the church. Accepting his invitation, the women dressed in their finest clothes and drove him to the church. When they arrived, they found the assistant pastor preparing a sermon. There was no reason for alarm as Elldredge told him that he wanted to show the church to the ladies. After the pastor left, Elldredge took the women into the basement, bound and blindfolded the female friend, and slaughtered the object of his hate. Afterward, he took the witness of his crime to his apartment, allegedly raped her, and set her free.

Bizarre events followed. When arrested, Elldredge pled guilty, confessed the evil within himself, and asked to die. During the next three years, he never wavered from his request, and on August 28, 2001, at midnight, he died by lethal injection without asking forgiveness but claiming that he was forgiven. His path to death, however, was strewn with victims, not only the witness to the murder, the family of the victim, and his wife but also the Lighthouse Free

Methodist Church itself. Headlines on the morning after his execution reported that he not only murdered a woman but killed a church as well. Even after the parishioners held a cleansing service in the rooms and around the sanctuary, neighbors refused to send their children to the daycare center and the ministry had to be closed. More tragic, the witness to the crime sued the church for negligence. When the layman who originally befriended James Elldredge in prison was asked to comment, he answered, "It did change the church, I guess, but it hasn't changed our goals. . . . Our goal is to reach out to people in need. . . . All the things that Jesus did for people did not turn out good for him, either." Then the pastor summed it up by saying, "The church was just being a church, reaching out to someone in need."

"Compassion fatigue" is a term that is often applied to burned-out social workers. "Redemption fatigue" is a term that has been introduced with disgust for public leaders who stonewall the truth about their misdeeds. When the church is *the* Church, its goal of compassion will not burn out and its acts of redemption will not die out.

21ST-CENTURY LEADERSHIP INITIATIVES

Anyone who believes in personal holiness also believes in social holiness. The two are never disconnected, and they inevitably interact. Some movements overemphasize one side or the other, and some even isolate one from the other. But these attempts are contrary to the great commandments and the teachings of Christ. Moreover, they represent triumphs for the intrusion of the Radical Self. Thus as we think forward to the agenda for Christian leadership in the 21st century, any plans for the witness of social holiness must be consistent with its companion of personal holiness and equally consistent with the principles of compassion taught by Jesus Christ.

1. **We must fairly provide for the welfare of every member of the family of God.** No one who is a brother or sister in the church should be destitute. Some churches have committees with the sole responsibility of monitoring the needs of the congregation and responding to them. In such cases, the compassion of the New Testament Church lives again and the church itself is blessed. A growing church, particularly as it diversifies, will have the special challenge not only of welcoming people of different races, ethnic backgrounds, and social classes into the family but also of expanding the resources of compassion for the diversity of needs that will come with them.

2. We must give relief without discrimination to our neighbors. One of the sad commentaries of the contemporary church is to learn about "drive-in" congregations whose members live outside the neighborhood and bypass churches in their own community on the way to worship. The reasons for this decision are equally sad. The commuters are seeking the comfort zone of friends, social class, and economic standing. Behind their drive is the engine of self-interest.

It will take a revolution to change this pattern, but someone must try. The starting point will be the church that defines its neighborhood as its neighbor and provides relief without discrimination for those needs. Going beyond those boundaries will add the challenge of relief without discrimination. In every case, the primacy of the need must take precedence over the selection of the recipient. "Who is my neighbor?" is a spiritual question that must be asked in every session where the vision, mission, and strategy of the church are discussed. To ask the right question will lead to the right answer.

3. We must give our enemies their rights without retaliation. Despite the way in which they treat us, our enemies are human beings created in the image of God and endowed with certain inalienable rights. Because they are human, we must love them, and because they are redeemable, we must pray for them. Whether those enemies are individuals or institutions, we cannot be agents of vengeance. Moreover, we are called to be the witnesses of grace and truth at one and the same time.

All of the tensions of paradox collapse on us when it comes to dealing with our enemies. On the one hand, they may reject biblical truth and give themselves over to the principalities and powers that rule the air. But on the other hand, they are people God has called us to love, bless—including the doing of good deeds—and pray for. Such an agenda exceeds human capability. We see the limits of our love almost daily in the issues that divide us. Abortion, homosexuality, stem cell research, global warming, school vouchers, racial conflict, defense systems, health care, and AIDS are divisive issues that make adversaries within the church, the nation, and the world. Yet if the church is to be *the* Church, it must find a way to address these issues with grace and truth, love and mercy. Stop for just a moment, identify an enemy of the faith, and pray, "Lord, how can I love, bless, do good, and pray for the one who is so easy to hate?"

A Symbol for Our Century

Usually when we think about compassion, we draw a small circle around distant ministries with an emotional appeal to which we can make a donation. Social holiness, however, is up close and personal. Beginning with the welfare of our extended family, extending to the care of our needy neighbors, and reaching out with blessing to our bitter enemies, the risks are real and self-interest is the issue at stake. For our compassion to be wholly holy, the unconditional love of God must inspire all of our actions and interactions in every human relationship, whether at home or abroad.

In 18th-century England, Wesleyans ministered under the banner "Faith Working Through Love." We can hear the heartbeat of both personal and social holiness in these words. We can sense the power of both truth and grace.

Wesleyans in the 21st century also need a banner flying at the masthead of our ministry. It, too, must send the signal of personal and social holiness. It, too, must send the message of truth and grace. As a start toward that goal, I propose *"Passion for One; Compassion for All."* A troubled world is waiting and watching.

12 The Power of a Holy Alliance

 Wherever and whenever the Spirit of God touches down on earth, things are made whole. Conversely, whenever the Radical Self invades human experience, the promise is wholeness, but the result is a broken world. We have been exploring how these principles are at work in many different dimensions of Christian belief and behavior. Dare we extend our exploration to include the way we organize and operate our Wesleyan ministries? If so, we must begin with a disquieting reality.

A Fragmented Witness

The Secular Cycle of the Fourth Great Awakening is upon us. Coalitions are developing around salient social and moral issues on both the Right and the Left. In a new twist, the spiritual agenda of the Wesleyan movement has been co-opted in a search for holiness along both secular and religious avenues. As we have seen, the secular search is motivated by the desire for "self-actualization" —an elusive term that psychologists put at the top of their scales for personal maturity. This search is also joined with pseudospiritual philosophies, such as New Age, and with Eastern religions, such as Buddhism. On the religious side, "holiness" has come back on the agenda as a priority for Calvinist and Reformed leadership. Pentecostals and other charismatics are still players in the field, but with limited impact because of an emphasis upon personal gifts more than social holiness.

What is the role of Wesleyans in the midst of this spiritual search? If the bottom line is drawn, we are at best bit players in a drama where we should be speaking from center stage. After all, who has a richer heritage in biblical holiness as belief, being, becoming, and behavior than Wesleyans? Why, then, are we only bit players? One answer may be the fragmentation of our witness. Is it possible that self-interest, like a worm contaminating a computer system, has infected our ministries and kept us apart?

While we contend for personal holiness, we must also

contend for spiritual and functional unity in our witness. Resounding in our ears are the great declarations of Ephesians—"one Lord, one faith, one baptism; one God and Father of [us] all" (4:5-6). Like the Ephesians, we make these confessions of faith and then promptly proceed to fragment the unity of our witness by the infusion of self-interest. Try this simple test. What is it that makes our Wesleyan witness weak in the current thrust for holiness? Certainly, it is not our position on biblical authority or fundamental differences in Wesleyan theology. Rather, it is such elements as history, governance, culture, and denominational identity that keep us small and weak. Consequently, our witness to biblical holiness suffers just when our voice is most urgently needed. It is time to ask whether or not organizational self-interest keeps us apart while at the same time we are trying to restore the meaning of self-sacrifice for our members.

A Double Fault

Missional fragmentation among Wesleyan denominations and institutions is being exposed in the 21st century by two demands upon our witness. The first is the *reality of globalization.* Although Wesleyans are known for their ministries in international missions, we still fall short of a whole worldview. In spirit we are global Christians, but in outlook we are still handicapped by a parochial view that makes America the center of the world. When translated into function, we organize around a Western viewpoint and operate by the models of Western culture. Consequently, we are global in name only and fall short of the oneness that Christ envisions for His Church.

The second fault that fragments our witness is seen at home and abroad. *We are strong at making converts, but woefully weak in developing disciples.* A comparison between the number of converts reported annually through local church ministries and the number of new members shows the problem at home. Internationally, the fault is compounded by mass conversions in third world countries where the resources for discipling ministries lag far behind.

The Wisdom of the Serpent

Jesus put His finger on our faults when He notes that the children of darkness are sometimes wiser than the children of light. He also advises us to be as wise as serpents and as harmless as doves. While not imitating the guile of serpents, we may have something to learn from them.

In a book titled *Blown to Bits* by Philip Evans and Thomas Wurster, the authors foresee the global challenge to the business world. In the past, businesses always had to make a compromise between "reach" and "richness." As a company extended its reach to potential customers, it had to sacrifice the richness of personal attention and product quality.[1] A one-stop supermarket versus a mom-and-pop grocery store serves as an example. The supermarket is geared to reaching new customers with volume buying and discount prices. A mom-and-pop corner grocery can only compete on the richness of personal attention, custom cuts, and money-back quality. Extend that image to the global scene. A worldwide reach is the ultimate test of richness. Globalization is blowing to bits the old business model.

Help is on the way. By the insertion of information technology into the breach between reach and richness, the gap is being closed. For the first time businesses do not have to make decisions based on compromise. The costly resources of physical plants and professional people do not have to be moved to distant sites in order to assure richness equal to the reach. To utilize the resources of high technology, however, strategic alliances in the form of consortia, partnerships, and mergers become the order of the day. Even "cobelligerents" in bitter competition find themselves needing each other. Competitive self-interest must be sacrificed for survival in the global marketplace.

Is there a message in the *Blown to Bits* model for the Wesleyan movement? If "reach" is interpreted as aggressive evangelism and "richness" means discipling for holiness, we have much to learn. Facts from home and abroad leave no doubt. In striving to be faithful to the Great Commission, we, too, have been impaled on the horns of the "reach" versus "richness" dilemma. As you read the mission statements of Wesleyan churches and institutions, the balance between evangelizing and discipling is readily apparent. In practice, however, the balance tips toward evangelizing. Looking back once again to the primary thrusts of recent decades, we see evangelistic crusades in the 1950s, personal evangelism in the 1960s, church growth in the 1970s, church planting in the 1980s, and church marketing in the 1990s. While our intentions are good, the Great Commission is only partially fulfilled. Converts do not know what they believe and do not behave much differently than their secular counterparts. The fault does not lie with them. Until we are as intentional in our discipling as we are in our evangelizing, the frustrating fallout between converts and members will continue. Somehow we must find a way to utilize the resources of information technology to help close the gap. We cannot do it alone. Our cost is too great, our expertise is too limited, and our time is too short. Strategic alliances among Wesleyan organizations and with other evangelical ministries must be explored. While information technology is not an instant answer, it is a beginning. Until we find a "breakout" option, the dilemma will remain. Wesleyan leaders need to explore every option that might help close the gap between reach and richness.

21st-Century Leadership Initiatives

When self-interest is put aside, multiple options for cooperation open up for us. If holiness is wholeness for institutions as well as individuals, we will actively search for these options.

1. **Wesleyan Leadership Summit.** The current emphasis on leadership development tends to be inner directed. As a means of church growth, leaders are identified and developed within the church. In turn, they are expected to develop other leaders in an expanding circle of a growing church. We must not forget the other dimension of leadership. Our leaders, especially in key positions of our churches, are expected to be out in front anticipating contemporary trends and exploring options for responding to those trends.

Globalization is one of those trends. Another is urbanization. Ray Bakke, our leading Evangelical urbanologist, often quotes, "The twentieth century is the first since the fifth century that Christianity has become a non-Western religion. . . . In 1900, over 80 percent of all Christians in the world were white, Western, and Northern, living in Europe or North America. By 1980, more than half of the world's Christians were nonwhite, non-Northern, and non-Western."[2] Paralleling the global shift is urban development. Bakke also cites the fact that "nearly three billion of the earth's six billion persons live in cities, the other three billion are being urbanized as well."[3]

When John Wesley announces "The world is my parish," he opens the globe for all future generations. Wesley's horse-ridden circuit has become our electronic circuit. As he reaches out his hand to all who share his faith and vision, we must reach out to all who enlarge and enrich our mission. The 21st-century challenge to Wesleyan leaders is to come together to explore the potential of cooperation for such needs as

- a global strategy for the Church in mission
- a united voice for biblical holiness on the domestic scene
- a theological think tank among Wesleyan scholars
- an understanding of the potential of informational technology in ministry

As you will note, a global strategy for the Church in mission is first on the agenda. The Wesleyan movement needs a paradigm shift that is nothing short of a paradigm bust. By vision and verb, we are out on the front edge of the future. By fact and function, we are someplace between the modes of survival and maintenance. At best, our challenge to the changing contemporary world is spotty. We will continue to limp along until we change our paradigm of ministry. Maintenance must give way to mission. When we make the shift, the goal, boundaries, and rules of ministry all change. In the ministry of maintenance, we protect the goal, limit the boundaries, and follow the rules of survival. But in the ministry of mission, we penetrate the culture, extend the boundaries, and let soul winning set the rules. With both reach and richness in mind, a Wesleyan summit needs to explore the paradigm of ministry that makes

- every nation a mission field
- every church a mission station
- every member a missionary

Perhaps in this perspective we will find the apostolic movement for which we have so long worked and waited. With a change of paradigm, a revolution is in the making.

Out of the leadership summit should come recommendations for task forces that are charged with the responsibility for exploring specific areas of cooperation and collaboration. Information technology, for instance, is a resource for evangelism and education filled with mystery and magic for most of us. Yet within our ranks are persons who have gifts and skills to master the mystery and capture the magic. The potential of such persons has already been demonstrated in the high-tech world of the Pacific Northwest. To put their faith into action, a group of young Microsoft "techies" set up a foundation for equipping, installing, and activating a computer network for International Child Care Ministries around the world. Rather than just sending equipment and money, teams from the foundation fly to those sites to do the work and become directly involved in missions.

Wesleyan literature is another need that has been highlighted on a global scale. In a recent letter to Wesleyan leaders, Jack Graves, special assistant to the president of Overseas Council, appeals for the publication of Wesleyan works in non-Western seminaries of the world. Graves cites the fact that in the global directory of 5,800 graduate schools of theology, only 18 (9 percent) are Wesleyan and non-Western. Of the 61 non-Western seminaries offering doctoral degrees, only two (3 percent) are Wesleyan and only one is Evangelical. As a person with a Wesleyan heritage who has visited scores of Evangelical seminaries around the world, Jack Graves pleads with the family he loves:

> I am encouraging leaders of Wesleyan missions and denominations to take this matter seriously. Unless these organizations become intentional about working more closely together to develop a presence at this critical level of leadership development for the non-Western world, it is difficult to be optimistic about the future of the Wesleyan family as a significant influence either in global evangelism or Christian education.
>
> At the same time I am encouraging leaders in the Wesleyan world to become much more intentional about the publication of text and reference books that are foundational to an understanding of Scripture from the Wesleyan perspective. I am doing this not out of blind loyalty to "*Wesleyanism*," (I belong to a nondenominational church) but because I believe it is a *Biblical* perspective and one that is greatly needed not only for Church health but Church growth in the non-Western world.[4]

With a vision like this for the needs of the world, we can see multiple opportunities coming out of a Wesleyan leadership summit. Imagine Wesleyan denominations and institutions coming together and wrapping their arms around the world with the message of holiness and hope. The energy of our faith, the vitality of our love, and the enlistment of our experts bring the sight of a world parish fully into view.

2. Strategic Alliances for Cooperation. Out of the strength of Wesleyan collaboration and cooperation, we can take the risk of entering into strategic alliances not only with other Evangelical groups but even with those we may identify as former cobelligerents. In the early 1990s, a controversial coalition of Evangelical Christians, conservative Roman Catholics, and modern Orthodox Jews was formed. Despite theological differences that will not and should not be resolved, the three parties stood together on the unshakeable ground that absolute truth was revealed by God in Holy Scripture. Just a generation ago, these three religious groups were bitter enemies. But in an age of moral relativism, they came together to stand against a common enemy. Evangelicals who signed the agreement were ostracized within their own community. This should not be. If we have the confidence we claim in our biblically based belief, we can cooperate with others for a common cause without lapsing into religious syncretism. From a position of strength, we can contribute to a voice that must be heard in the larger society. This same conviction took me into such positions as being an officer in the National Religious Partnership for the Environment headed by Al Gore and Carl Sagan. Ronald Sider and I, representing Evangelicals in that partnership, were able to keep biblical truth in balance with environmental activism and also gain the respect of our Jewish, Roman Catholic, and Liberal Protestant partners. For me, the memorable moment came after Carl Sagan and I became friends. At lunch one day, he told me that while he publicly professed his atheism, there were private moments when he had doubts about his position. I prayed for him until the day of his death.

Still another unforgettable experience came to me as a vice president of the North American section of the World Methodist Council. Under the aegis of our Wesleyan heritage, Methodists from around the world come together to preserve their roots and advance their cause. But within that context, delegates can range from vigorous advocates of Wesleyan sanctification to equally vigorous proponents of liberal theology, feminism, and homosexuality. Debates are always lively, and politics are always rampant, but the voice of biblical truth is never stifled. At the World Methodist Council quadrennial meeting in Nairobi, Kenya, in 1986, I shared the plenary platform with the head of the World Council of Churches. Taking the theme seriously, I gave a biblical message on the subject "Jesus Christ, Our Only Hope for Salvation." Later, the leader of the World Council of Churches took the position that there were many roads to God and Christians needed to open their arms to embrace other religions in a pluralistic world. A press conference in which we both participated sent two different messages around the world. From that experience came the conviction that if we have full confidence in our biblical message, we can take our witness into the white-hot crucible of holy alliances and cobelligerent coalitions without being cowed or compromised.

3. A World Wesleyan Fellowship. What is the critical mass of Wesleyan resources needed to impact the world on a global scale and contribute significantly to the continuing quest for holiness?

Our history records an encounter between Methodist Episcopal leaders and Bishop Francis Asbury back in the late 18th century. Rather than staying on the East Coast where Methodism was strong, Asbury vowed to follow the call of God and travel by horseback over the Appalachian Mountains to evangelize the Western frontier that stretched to the Mississippi River. His colleagues in leadership warned him about the sparse prospects, saying, "If you go, you will be able to count all of the Methodists in a corn crib." Asbury countered, "I will show you the way."

His leadership is legendary. Francis Asbury crossed the Appalachians 60 times, logged over 270,000 miles on horseback, recruited an army of 1,000 circuit riders, evangelized the Western frontier, and made Methodism a moral as well as spiritual force that united East and West under the watchword "One Nation Under God."

Our 21st century calls for the same bold and visionary leadership to show us the way. Among the options some have considered is denominational merger. If we are in the "postdenominational" period of our history, dare we hang on to an outmoded structure?—unless our theological and missional integrity is sacrificed by change. Dale Earnhardt, the legendary race car driver, died when he refused to wear an advanced safety harness designed especially for the type of crash that killed him. A commentator who had followed Earnhardt through his career said, "Dale Earnhardt had one fault. He failed to adjust to the progress he had advanced."

Christian leaders can be guilty of the same fault. After advancing the Church with vision and energy, we can lose our own momentum while the Church moves on. Periodically, we must ask whether or not our structures are dragging on our mission. As heirs of John Wesley, we have our pattern. Without compromising his theological integrity, he created structures that moved with his mission. What would Wesley say about our denominational structures today? We know he would not recommend that Wesleyan denominations merge for the sake of size or power. But if merger means the advancement of mission, I suspect he would be the first to take the lead.

Merger is not the only alternative for a world Wesleyan fellowship. As always in organizational development, form must follow function. Other options may well be more consistent with the changing needs of the 21st century. We will never know unless we try. If the Wesleyan message is a truth whose time has come once again, we dare not miss the opportunity.

THE WITNESS OF ONENESS

Returning to our original thought for this chapter, we have extended the meaning of holiness and wholeness to structural and organizational relationships. The Radical Self delights in keeping Christians fragmented, individually and institutionally. In the past, the fragmentation has given the fabric of faith its richness. Today, as the globe shrinks along with our resources, it is our weakness. Therefore, rather than withdrawing into ourselves, we should be asking how we can work together to fulfill Wesley's dream of a world parish. Our leaders must be given the encouragement and freedom to explore every option. The potential for holy alliance is limited only by the size of our spiritual vision.

Epilogue
Our Living Hope

Return with me to the story of the Seattle earthquake. As news flashes interrupted regular TV programming, we learned that an earthquake that measured 7.3 on the Richter scale had hit us. The epicenter was 60 miles away in the capitol city of Olympia, Washington. Except for the fact that the eruption occurred 30 miles deep in the earth, the damage in dollars and the cost of lives might well have been the greatest in human history. As it was, the damage totaled more than 100 million dollars, primarily due to the collapse of structures or infrastructures that predated newer building codes. Next to the rubble of old walls and crevices in old roadways, skyscrapers rising 76 stories in the air escaped with nothing more than shifting items on the tops of desks. Thanks to advanced engineering, they rolled with the shock and then settled back into their natural sway.

After the earthquake, two words were heard over and over again—"anticipation" and "preparation." Scientists admitted the fallibility of the instruments in detecting earthquakes in advance. They also agreed that preparation—such as building codes—could limit damage but not assure an earthquakeproof environment. Bowing before the potential power and the uncertain timing of natural forces beyond their control, they could only declare, "A major earthquake will hit Seattle. The question is not "If?" but "When?"

The more I learned about the earthquake, the more I thought about the second coming of Jesus Christ. Although the event will be a disaster only for those who have rejected Christ, the watchwords are the same for all of us—"anticipation" and "preparation." We anticipate the Second Coming as our living hope and prepare for the event as our daily discipline. Like the scientist's prediction of an earthquake, the question for the Second Coming is not "If?" but "When?" With that same certainty about the event and the same uncertainty about the timing, our leaders must show us the way.

KILLER OF HOPE

The Radical Self undermines our desire for hope and wrecks havoc with our timing. Millions of people inspired by self-interest hope for self-actualization. In truth, however, their goal is elusive, and more often than not, hope becomes despair. The signs are all around us. Our children are the first victims. When parents substitute money for love, children can catch the disease coined as "affluenza" with all of the symptoms of impoverishment, including drugs, crime, violence, and even suicide. Young adults are also unwitting victims of self-interest. When asked whether they are optimistic or pessimistic about the future, they tend to answer they are optimistic for their lives but pessimistic about society. These trends come to fruition in adults who are pursuers of success, status, and security in the name of self-interest. They experience "anomie," a psychological term used to describe the free-floating anxiety of persons who have no anchor in morals or meaning to hold them steady. Senior citizens, migrating to Southern climes, assume they have paid their dues and deserve the comforts of self during their retirement years. Like the sirens in the sails of Ulysses' craft, the wooing of the Radical Self is a dead end freighted with disaster. Self-interest cannot survive without a short-term view for the future and a shorter memory of the past.

All of the deadly symptoms of the Radical Self were exposed on September 11, 2001. Arrogance gave way to personal anxiety, security gave way to national fear, and affluence gave way to economic uncertainty. In a moment of time, we saw the thin veil of our hope for the future rent from top to bottom. Temporarily, at least, our dependence shifted from the Radical Self to the holy God. We can be sure that the Radical Self will not give up. For the moment it may appear to be beaten, but without redemption by death, it lives to fight again. The time frame is short and the window of opportunity is small. We dare not miss the opportunity to remind the world that our only hope is in the Christ of the holy God.

CHRIST, THE HOPE OF GLORY

The biblical view of hope stands in sharp contrast with the false promise of the Radical Self. Leaders in the Word of God are constantly leaning into the future with high anticipation. Whether it is the prophets of the Old Testament expecting the Messiah, the disciples of Jesus waiting for Pentecost, the apostle Paul urging the churches to look for the Second Coming, or John the Revelator foreseeing a new heaven and a new earth, their words are radiant with hope and charged with expectancy.

Hope, the Believer's Inheritance. Christians of the 21st century are heirs of hope. True to the promise of Christ, the Holy Spirit shows us "things to come." Like looking through the big end of a telescope, we see a future of hope in which we have a significant and meaningful role to play. We are not to be giddy dreamers, cock-eyed optimists, or "minimessiahs." But we will join with God's faithful people of all ages who have never given up hope or given in to despair. With them, we sing, "Praise be to the God and Father of our Lord Jesus Christ! In his great mercy he has given us new birth into a living hope through the resurrection of Jesus Christ from the dead" (1 Pet. 1:3).

Once we know the source of our inheritance, we can understand why New Testament writers reach for superlatives to describe our "living hope." In Rom. 12:12, we are "joyful in hope." In Titus 2:13, the author speaks of "blessed hope." And in the monumental passage of Col. 1:27, we see "Christ . . . the hope of glory." This is our biblical heritage.

Hope, the Leader's Gift. Although our hope is grounded in the resurrection of Christ, encouraged by the Scriptures, and confirmed by reason, it is still the point of attack by the forces of despair. Christian leaders have a special responsibility to keep hope alive among their people. First, *our leaders are responsible for keeping hope alive during times of turmoil and trouble.* Along with the church at Colossae, we need to be constantly reminded that "faith and love . . . spring from the hope that is stored up for [us] in heaven" (Col. 1:5). We also need to see "hope as an anchor for the soul, firm and secure" (Heb. 6:19). Here we may think of the image of stormy seas threatening to capsize a ship or run it aground. Only a sea anchor can save the day. Christian leaders serve as that anchor during times of crisis, conflict, and transition. Our outlook must be hopeful and our actions must be consistent with hope. If leaders lose hope, all lose hope.

Second, *our leaders must see hope as a companion of holiness.* Hope is not usually considered one of the spiritual disciplines. But in 1 John 3:2-3, we read, "Dear friends, now we are children of God, and what we will be has not yet been made known. But we know that when he appears, we shall be like him, for we shall see him as he is. Everyone who has this hope in him purifies himself, just as he is pure." The greater our hope in Christ, the greater our desire to be like Him. To be faithful to their calling, Christian leaders will keep the vision of seeing Christ fresh in the minds of their people and, by purifying themselves, keep the anticipation alive.

Third, *our leaders must exemplify the patience of hope while we await His coming.* Waiting for the "blessed hope" created a great tension for early Christian leaders, especially the apostles. With the vision of the ascending Christ still in their eyes and the promise of His return still echoing in their ears, they had to balance the immediacy of His return with the reality of waiting. Rom. 8 draws an unforgettable comparison between creation waiting with "eager expectation for the sons of God to be revealed" and the newly redeemed waiting "eagerly" for their "adoption as sons [and] the redemption of [their] bodies" (vv. 19, 23).

A similar paradox looms ahead for 21st-century Christian leaders. How do we "wait with eager expectation" at one and the same time? The tendency is to lapse into the indolence of waiting or rush into the anxiety of expecting. As the New Testament writers have the mind of the Spirit in keeping the balance between the present and the future, our leaders for the 21st century must have this same mind. How do we wait for the Second Coming with eager expectation?

BRING IN THE CANDLES!

During my junior high school days, I was introduced to a poem by John Greenleaf Whittier titled "Abraham Davenport." No poetry has had a greater impact upon my view of the Second Coming. Even though it is written in verse, it spells out what "waiting with eager expectation" means for us today.

In 1780, New England suddenly fell under a shroud of darkness during the middle of the day. The cry went up that the great day of the Lord had come, and fear gripped the people as they waited for the "doom blast of the trumpet." Some fell to their knees in repentance, and others rushed to the hills to await His coming. In the old state house of Connecticut, the legislature was in session debating a minor bill regulating alewives of the fishing industry. When the darkness fell, the lawgivers also panicked. "It is the Lord's Great Day! Let us adjourn," they cried as they quaked in their boots. Only Abraham Davenport remained calm and with a steady voice "cleaved the intolerable hush":

"This well may be
The Day of Judgment which the world awaits;
But be it so or not, I only know
My present duty, and my Lord's command
To occupy till He come. So at the post
Where He hath set me in His providence,
I choose, for one, to meet Him face-to-face,—
No faithless servant frightened from my task,
But ready when the Lord of the harvest calls;
And therefore, with all reverence, I would say,
Let God do His work, we will see to ours.
Bring in the candles."
And they did.[1]

While Abraham Davenport represents the Spirit-guided balance between waiting and working, the Bible gives an edge to watching with "eager expectation." The ring of expectancy must be a vibrant chord resounding throughout the Christian community. It is a distant chord sounding the promise of the Second Coming. It is a current chord resonating with anticipation for the visitation of the Holy Spirit.

WAIT, WORK, AND WATCH

Wesleyan leaders are spiritual optimists as well as reasonable enthusiasts. Our hope-filled outlook is grounded in the revelation that the Holy Spirit is still at work in the world and the fact that He is the Master of surprise. Some theologies try to explain every contingency, resolve every paradox, and control every circumstance. Wesleyans, however, are people whose faith in the dynamic work of the Holy Spirit gives us the freedom to follow His leadership rather than do His work for Him. Who can predict how the Holy Spirit will fulfill Jesus' promise that He will lead us into all truth, convict the world of sin, righteousness, and judgment, and show us things to come? Wesleyans may be criticized for revivalism, enthusiasm, perfectionism, and pietism, but we are also known for being open, ready, and willing to welcome the visitation of the Holy Spirit.

I found this spirit of eager expectation alive and well during my presidency at Asbury Theological Seminary. The graduate school is located in a small village nestled up against Appalachia and far from the maddening urban crowd. At first, I wanted to figure out how to move the seminary into the realities of the contemporary world. But then I read its history and became engulfed in its spirit. As a regular stopover on the frontier and camp-meeting circuit of Francis Asbury during the early 19th century, Wilmore, Kentucky, received a legacy of spiritual anticipation that is passed on to students from generation to generation. Even today, chapels of the seminary and college are filled to capacity as a symbol of readiness for the Spirit of God to be poured out upon all flesh.

My experience in speaking at scores of Evangelical colleges and conferences confirms this observation about the Wesleyan spirit of expectancy. Watching with eager expectation distinguishes Wesleyans worldwide. Whether in our personal, congregational, or denominational outlook, we are open, willing, and ready for the visitation of the Holy Spirit. Such expectancy is not another form of narcissism designed to bolster our collective egos. It is essential to the survival of our society. A Great Awakening takes a full generation to influence the moral tone of a culture. But during that same period, counterforces arise to twist and corrupt its redemptive impulse. Our generation of Wesleyan leaders carries the responsibility to keep the spirit of awakening alive. We can survive only so long on the borrowed spiritual capital of the past. Whether living in the midst of the Fourth Great Awakening or leading on the front edge of the Fifth Great Awakening, our task is to hold out the realistic hope of continuing renewal. Holy expectancy is one of the gifts of biblical holiness to each generation.

Keep Your Forks!

Ann Landers has never been the source for a closing thought for my sermons or books—until now. My wife reads Ann Landers along with Billy Graham each morning in the newspaper. Occasionally, she will call to my attention a letter written to Ann Landers. It is a wonderful way for a wife to get her point across. Recently, she asked me to read a letter to Ann that sums up what I have been trying to say about the gift of holy expectancy. The letter told the story of a woman who asked her pastor if she could be buried with a fork in her hand. Of course the pastor said she could have her wish, but curiosity prompted him to ask why. The woman answered, "At our family table, when my mother told us to keep our forks, we knew that something good was coming. When I die, I want everyone to know that the best is yet to come."

What better way to convey the wholeness of hope that God has reserved for His holy people! We have the text for our message in the promise of God; we have the tone for our message in the grace note of hope. If "watching with eager expectation" resounds through our message in the 21st century, we will be partners with the Holy Spirit in setting the tone for God's redemptive work. Leaning into the future, let us embrace this total truth:

> With love, we *wait;*
> With faith, we *work;* and
> With hope, we *watch.*

> To God be the glory!

Notes

Prologue

1. John Wesley, *The Works of John Wesley*, ed. Edward H. Sugden (Grand Rapids: Francis Asbury Press, 1955), 11:384.

2. John Wesley, *A Plain Account of Christian Perfection*, ed. Albert C. Outler (Oxford: Oxford University Press, 1964), 275.

3. Robert N. Bellah et al., *Habits of the Heart* (Berkeley, Calif.: University of California Press, 1985), 335.

4. Philip Yancey, "Living with Furious Opposites," *Christianity Today*, 4 September 2000, 70-78.

5. C. L. Franklin, quotation from *Seattle Post-Intelligencer* editorial column.

Chapter 1

1. Max DePree, *Leadership Is an Art* (New York: Bantam Doubleday Dell Publishing Group, 1989), 11.

2. Nathan Hatch, *The Democratization of the American Christianity* (New Haven, Conn.: Yale University Press, 1989), 5.

3. Robert William Fogel, *The Fourth Great Awakening and the Future of Egalitarianism* (Chicago: University of Chicago Press, 2000).

4. Ibid., 2-3.

Chapter 2

1. Timothy Smith, *Revivalism and Social Reform* (New York: Abingdon Press, 1957), 148-77.

2. William McLoughlin, *Revivalism, Awakenings, and Reform* (Chicago: University of Chicago Press, 1978), 141.

3. Anthony F. C. Wallace, "Revitalization Movements: Some Theoretical Considerations for Their Comparative Study," *American Anthropology* 58 (1956): 264-65.

4. Richard Lovelace, *Dynamics of Spiritual Life: An Evangelical Theology of Renewal* (Downers Grove, Ill.: InterVarsity Press, 1979), 79.

5. Howard Snyder, *Signs of the Spirit* (Grand Rapids: Zondervan, 1989), 61-62.

6. Fogel, *The Fourth Great Awakening and the Future of Egalitarianism*, 95.

7. Neil Howe and William Strauss, *The Fourth Turning: An American Prophecy* (New York: Broadway Books, 1997), 3.

Chapter 3

1. Elton Trueblood, *The New Man for Our Time* (New York: Harper and Row Publishers, 1970), 126.

Chapter 4

1. Lyle Schaller, *21 Bridges to the 21st Century* (Nashville: Abingdon Press, 1944), 133-42.
2. Howe, *The Fourth Turning*, 3.
3. David Van Biema, "New Lights of the Spirit," *Time*, 11 December 2000.

Chapter 5

1. Karl Menninger, *Whatever Happened to Sin?* (New York: Hawthorn Books, 1973).
2. Elie Wiesel, *Parade Magazine*, 28 October 2000, 4-5.
3. Charles Colson, "Wake-up Call," *Christianity Today*, 12 November 2001, 112.

Chapter 6

1. A. W. Tozer, preface to *The Knowledge of the Holy* (New York: HarperCollins Publishers, 1961), vii.
2. J. I. Packer, preface to *Knowing God* (Downers Grove, Ill.: InterVarsity, 1993), 12.
3. Donald Bloesch, "Whatever Happened to God?" *Christianity Today*, 5 February 2001, 54-55.
4. Tozer, *The Knowledge of the Holy*, vii.
5. Ibid.
6. Ibid., 105.
7. H. Richard Niebuhr, *The Kingdom of God in America* (Middletown, Conn.: Wesleyan University Press, 1937), 193.
8. Tozer, *The Knowledge of the Holy*, vii.
9. Ibid.

Chapter 7

1. James I. Packer, *Keep in Step with the Spirit* (Old Tappan, N.J.: Fleming H. Revell, 1984), 93-115.
2. Lewis A. Drummond, *The Evangelist* (Nashville: Word Publishing, 2001), 19.
3. Ibid.
4. Ibid.
5. Ibid., 20.
6. Charles Colson, *Born Again* (Grand Rapids: Fleming H. Revell, 1976), 314-16.
7. R. C. Sproul, *The Holiness of God* (Wheaton, Ill.: Tyndale House Publishers, 1985), 3-5.
8. Ibid., 6.
9. Ibid., 12.
10. Henri J. M. Nouwen, *In the Name of Jesus* (New York: Crossroad, 1991), 13-73.

Chapter 8

1. Marva Dawn, *Keeping the Sabbath Wholly* (Grand Rapids: William B. Eerdmans, 2000), 69.
2. Ibid., 203-11.
3. Ibid., 137.
4. Ibid., 63-64.

Chapter 10

1. Fogel, *The Fourth Great Awakening,* 170-71.

2. George Hunter, *Challenge in Evangelism Today* 34, No. 1 (spring/summer 2001).

3. Michael Hamilton, "We're in the Money!" *Christianity Today,* 12 June 2000, 36-43.

4. Norman Edwards, comments made at Asbury Theological Seminary in 1991.

Chapter 12

1. Philip Evans and Thomas Wurster, *Blown to Bits* (Boston: Harvard Business School Press, 2000), 23-38.

2. Raymond Bakke, *A Biblical Word for an Urban World* (Valley Forge, Pa.: Board of International Ministries, American Baptist Churches U.S.A., 2000), 1.

3. Raymond Bakke, *A Theology As Big as the City* (Downers Grove, Ill.: Inter-Varsity Press, 1997), 12.

4. Jack Graves, vice president for communications, personal letter to the Advisory Committee of Overseas Council.

Epilogue

1. John Greenleaf Whittier, *The Poetical Works of Whittier,* ed. Hyatt Waggoner, Cambridge ed. (Boston: Houghten Mifflin Company, 1975), 259.